D1141273

BLOOMING DUBLIN

Blooming DUBLIN

Choice, Change and Contradictions

ANNE SIMPSON

MAINSTREAM
PUBLISHING

EDINBURGH AND LONDON

IN MEMORY OF MY PARENTS
whose love of Dublin was infectious

First published in Great Britain 1991 by
MAINSTREAM PUBLISHING COMPANY (EDINBURGH) LTD
7 Albany Street
Edinburgh EH1 3UG

ISBN 1 85158 324 6 (cloth)

A catalogue record for this book is available from the British Library

Photographs by Colin McPherson
Author photograph by James Morrison
Typeset in 11/13 Times by Blackpool Typesetting Services Ltd
Printed in Great Britain by Mackays of Chatham

ACKNOWLEDGMENTS

IN THE MONTHS that we have travelled together for the purposes of this book Dublin has proved a fascinating, passionate, infuriating, mysterious and endlessly generous companion. So, much of my thanks must go to the city itself but I am also indebted to scores of people who, with immediate kindness and enthusiasm, gave me so much of their time and knowledge and, in many cases, went to considerable trouble to put me in touch with others equally helpful, enlightening and forthcoming. Although reference is made to various scholarly titles (details are given at the back of the book), this is not an academic study. Nor, I hope, is it a coffee-table book. It is, instead, a work of journalism inspired by the experience of covering news assignments in Dublin over the past 12 years, and drawn together here in the form of interviews and impressionistic essays.

There simply is not space to thank individually all those who helped, but they have my enduring gratitude. John Cooney, formerly with the *Irish Times* and now with the European Commission in Brussels, was the first to open his contacts book to me and no fellow journalist can receive a more gallant gift. Similarly warm thanks must go to Rosaleen Linehan and Ita McAuliffe who, early on, put me on the trail of Mary Robinson's rolling and eventually momentous campaign for the Presidency. My lasting thanks, too, in those weeks go to Dr Aubrey Bourke, Mary Harney, Dermot Bolger and Paul Durcan. My thanks also to Peter Pearson, Jim Sheridan, Peter Sheridan, Gay Byrne, Bernard Treacy, Garret FitzGerald, Rita Childers and the late John Kelly for their insights, humour and ready co-operation. And I shall always be grateful to Charlie and Mariad Whisker for the quality and sensitivity of their perceptions on the enduring agonies in the North. Others who allowed me to poach their valuable time were John and Odette Rocha, Michael Mortell, Paul Costelloe, Muriel McCarthy, Myrtle Zack, Brian Lenihan, Carmencita Hederman, Nuala Talbot, Aidan Kinch, Maureen Connolly, Robert Ballagh, Ciaran Benson, Susan Naughton, the staff at the National Library, and all those friends in Tallaght, especially Rose O'Keeffe and Bridie Sweeney who went to considerable trouble to ferry me around. John Brown, at Bord Failte, spent a rainy lunch hour helping me to check statue inscriptions, and in the unsavoury matter of Dalkey dog droppings Frank Burke proved an illuminating and funny sage. For her wisdom and incomparable fund of stories I owe enormous thanks to Maura Dunne. She along with my family and closest friends will never know how much their counsel and encouragement kept me sane, and so an abundance of thanks, too, to my sisters, Brigid, Stephanie and Claire, to Brendan, Sheila and Beattie O'Shea, Maura and Ted McSweeney, Kilian and Beatrice O'Sullivan, and especially to Fionnuala Dunne and David Roy for just being there with unstinting hospitality, kindness and good humour. In Scotland I am grateful to Harry Reid (deputy editor of the *Glasgow Herald*), Mainstream's Bill Campbell and Peter MacKenzie who set me forth on this adventure, to Penny Clarke and Judy Diamond, to Colin McPherson for being a most unobtrusively effective photographer, and also for the continual support I received from Eva Collins and my *Glasgow Herald* colleagues William Russell, Ann Shaw, William Hunter, Isabel Barnes and Anne Galloway. But none of the following pages would ever have made it to deadline without the gentle, masterful goading of Arnold Kemp who took on the the tireless role of amanuensis and head filleter with uncommon dexterity, good grace and wit. To him, my most profound thanks, and love.

CONTENTS

PROLOGUE

ON THE DAY that Stephen Roche finally spun his wheels to an Irish triumph in the Tour de France Mickey Dazzler lolled against his own particular racer perched on the kerb outside the Gresham Hotel. Earlier he had been wobbling and weaving through a sea-borne mist on the Vico Road, a pair of luminous orange tags whirling companionably around his spokes in warning of his rolling presence. To the mind of a stranger any man as old as Mickey Dazzler half way up a precipitous hillside on a bicycle had to be either a fool or a rogue trick cyclist on the rounds with Fossett's Circus. Mickey Dazzler, thin as a blade of grass, with his skin browned by tobacco and south-westerly tempests, was neither one nor the other of these things. By fate and habit he was the husband of one of Moore Street's market princesses, a woman whose voice was loud as America, and one who guarded her fruit and vegetable stall with a torrential gabble that could freeze the blood.

Now in his 68th year but still nippily possessed of a jockey's frame, Mickey Dazzler existed in the farthermost corner of his wife's haranguing reputation, and for this he had his bicycle to thank. To reach that safe haven a bike was vital for making those handy exits from marital fury. Once propelled the wheels were swift and silent, requiring no petrol money which, by some risky scheming, might, anyway, have to be rifled from the wife. It was Sunday, and the bicycle clips which gathered his trouser bottoms into neatly pleated cuffs, also drew attention to the old-fashioned shine of the Dazzler's shoes. His coat was a navy melton, not the newest but well enough kept to confirm that here was a man who believed in hanging up his clothes last thing at night. On his head he wore a pale grey fedora which, to his thinking, was the classiest hat in the

9

whole of Dublin. At its left side, for extra swank, a small red feather was tucked into the petersham band, and from the Dazzler's mouth an unlit cigarette dangled so permanently it might have been stitched to his lower lip.

Mickey Dazzler was the supreme example of how, in Ireland, humankind and the bicycle are inextricably one. Old men, young men, teachers and slewderers, blackguards, small girls, bishops' housekeepers and politicians' legmen all take to the saddle so readily that occasionally one wonders if they ever have a chance to sit down anywhere else. In city or town or on a ragged country track all are seen at one time or another, taking liberties with anything than might resemble a highway code or spinning contentedly by, their coats and day-glo capes spread out theatrically behind them. In Dublin now, however, there is a certain class of cyclist whose very appearance acts like a visual reprimand to the Porsche mentality of the flash-and-tan set. With his stout-stained bow tie, crumpled tweeds patched with leather through necessity rather than snobbery, and a pound of sausages strapped into the back satchel, such a biker incurs the kind of abuse and ridicule which only serves as a reminder to the cycling intelligentsia that in Ireland its name remains a dirty word. Pedalling intellectuals, their furious legs whipping bicycles onwards through the squalid wastes of prejudice and censorship, have found themselves accused of almost everything in Dublin from subversion to élitism, from being drunk in charge of a puncture kit to refusing the motorist's challenge to throw off the jacket and fight.

Long ago that literary illusionist, Flann O'Brien (in real life Brian O'Nolan but also known as the columnist Myles Na Gopaleen) lampooned such weaseled bigotry when he observed the mysterious interaction between man and the bicycle in his tragi-comic novel, *The Third Policeman*: 'The gross and net result of it is that people who spent most of their natural lives riding iron bicycles over the rocky roadsteads of this parish get their personalities mixed up with the personalities of their bicycles as the result of the interchanging of the atoms of each of them . . .' said the Sergeant. 'If you let it go too far it would be the end of everything. You would have bicycles wanting votes and then they would get seats on the county council and make the roads far worse than they are for their own ulterior motivation. But against that . . . there is a great deal of charm about it.'

PROLOGUE

That Sunday when Stephen Roche rode to victory, Mickey Dazzler bought his latest racer from a man who was selling a bunch of them outside Mount Jerome Cemetery at Harold's Cross. On the roof of his son-in-law's third-hand Granada he transported the new prize to Killiney Bay, then, coaxing the machine with a lifetime's expertise he made his way in stately fashion round the scenic curves until, with head lowered and shoulders hunched, he sped down the Vico as if possessed by the pedalling dementia of the Tour de France itself. The Dazzler already had one bike but this new model was different. Its handlebars possessed a champion's gleam and the kind of black perforated grips one associates with expensively tailored nappa gloves. The frame was shocking pink making it altogether the sort of bicycle which a Flann O'Brien character might tenderly lean 'against the dresser of a warm kitchen when it was pouring outside'. Of course, the Moore Street princess would never permit such licence at home, and, in its way, that was a good thing, for when a bike was kept beyond her line of vision, she didn't miss it when it joined in her husband's cunning escapes. And if she didn't miss the racer, then she didn't miss the Dazzler. That was the way of it, all right.

Back on O'Connell Street, perched on the Gresham's kerb, the Dazzler looked like a well-preened pigeon, the head jabbing the air in a circular motion to take in every corner of the scene. He revelled in these moments of repose when the passing world would gaze at him through its car window. Soon he would walk his bike up Westmoreland Street, then past Trinity College, with its mangle of scholastic cycles in the courtyard, and onwards along Grafton Street to Stephen's Green where he would rest it against railings while he inspected the calibre of visitor entering or leaving the Shelbourne Hotel. He would wheel his bike beside him, holding it by the handles as if he were guiding an old person through the park. And on reflection he wondered if that wasn't the way the two of them should travel now, himself and the racer moving in a gentle rhythm, attentively abreast. Oh, the downward speed of a vertical hill was thrilling, but at his age a man had to guard against stones. One malign pebble hitting the front tyre at a nasty angle and Mickey Dazzler could be thrown headfirst into a bramble hedge. A ruinous fate, that, for the classiest hat in town.

1

INTRODUCTION
Blooming Dublin

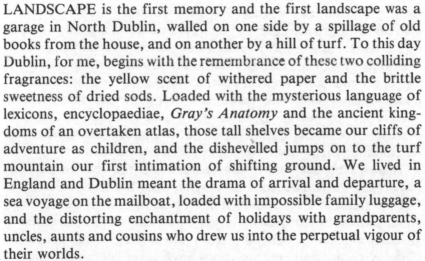

LANDSCAPE is the first memory and the first landscape was a garage in North Dublin, walled on one side by a spillage of old books from the house, and on another by a hill of turf. To this day Dublin, for me, begins with the remembrance of these two colliding fragrances: the yellow scent of withered paper and the brittle sweetness of dried sods. Loaded with the mysterious language of lexicons, encyclopaediae, *Gray's Anatomy* and the ancient kingdoms of an overtaken atlas, those tall shelves became our cliffs of adventure as children, and the dishevelled jumps on to the turf mountain our first intimation of shifting ground. We lived in England and Dublin meant the drama of arrival and departure, a sea voyage on the mailboat, loaded with impossible family luggage, and the distorting enchantment of holidays with grandparents, uncles, aunts and cousins who drew us into the perpetual vigour of their worlds.

At least that is how it seemed, for unlike the exhausted Britain of the Fifties Dublin always appeared to be in the thick of things. Around the supper table an uncle would recall setting out from the city in his student days at four in the morning to pedal the 220 miles to south-west Kerry on a bike. He was heading for the wedding of a sister, his good suit rolled up protectively (and no doubt disastrously) then strapped above the front wheel. A pile of books plus a bottle of embrocation were secured behind the saddle. 'To make sure the old saliva was doing its job on those first 20 miles I kept

13

a pebble in my mouth until Newbridge,' he would tell us. 'But by the time I reached the house in Kenmare the chin was down to my knees and I was the size of a threepenny bit.'

Today all has changed and yet not utterly. Mobility is still a curse, but it is more the mobility of emigration, the wrenching shame of a country that must rear children for departure lounges because no one can promise them a livelihood at home. But for almost 20 years the Republic itself has been in transit; on the move culturally, emotionally, spiritually and economically between the priggish absolutes of de Valera's homespun nationalism and the tilting priorities of a Europe suddenly re-drawn. Economic dependency kept Ireland shackled to Britain until both joined the Common Market in 1973, one bursting to get through the door, the other sulking on the threshold. 'Psychologically that was a breath of air for us,' recalls Brian Lenihan, who, from 1989 to the winter of 1990, was Fianna Fail deputy Prime Minister until his unseemly sacking by Charles Haughey. But with enrolment in Europe there also came the growing pains of an infant nation struggling to climb out of its isolated cradle and then finding itself socially at odds in the clubrooms of the member states. For Dublin's progressives the choice remains simple: either continue to pursue the kind of archaic conservatism that will make the Republic an international irrelevancy, or put its constitutional house in order, not only to place divorce on the statute books but to honour and substantiate its commitment to building bridges with the North.

Tensions between the traditionalists and the reconstructivists have raged for two decades, although among the former there is at last the tremor of realisation that Dublin will never woo back to Ireland those thousands of bright, graduate emigrants unless it sheds any lingering illiberal pietism and undergoes radical shifts. Change, choice and contradictions have never been more sharply etched into the psyche of the Republic than they are now, and it is those three words which provide the theme of this impressionistic study of Dublin, a city whose essential vitality, politics and pre-occupations, its informal air and gab and dedication to the arts compose so much of what is understood by the term, *Irish identity*. In some ways the Victorian red of Dublin makes it look more like London than any city in Britain, but in its moods and manner, and treasured flexibility concerning time, Dublin is as foreign to the British mind as Rome. Today, even when outraged, Dubliners make the most of a good grievance, lubricating it with an abundant flow of conversation. 'The Eastern by-pass . . .' groans a man on the bus to Sallynoggin, the object of his pain being a hotly contested plan to sink a motorway beneath Sandymount's fabled strand. 'Honest to God, I'll tell you this: I've lived in Dublin all my days yet the more I see of the place the less I understand it.'

Traffic has always driven Dublin into preposterous bottlenecks, for the physical size of its streets and the intimate higgle-piggle of much of its domestic architecture are made more for the short circuit than for the bumper-to-bumper snarl-up caused by the present's endless rushing. Long ago Dublin should have perished from the fearful pall of fumes pumped out by its buses, or else succumbed to nerves and gone off its rocker from the daily traffic diversions caused by sudden craters in the road. Yet Dublin always manages to extricate itself from self-destruction by some lucky wisecrack, meeting confusion and congestion with patience, drollery and grit. The novelist William Trevor recalls his father, a native of Cork, visiting Dublin in the Thirties and driving the wrong way down Grafton Street whereupon he met a guard on point duty at the other end. 'Ah, sure you got here,' said the policeman, 'and isn't that the main thing.' Somewhere among the anecdotes in *No Laughing Matter*, that fine biography of the writer Flann O'Brien, the book's author Anthony Cronin remembers a story which defines precisely the Dublin art of muddling through. O'Brien, whose real name was Brian O'Nolan, was occasionally maladroit in traffic and one day when he was driving along Eden Quay towards O'Connell Street he was waved to the side of the road by a robust pointsman. As is the custom in such situations the guard took his time in walking over to O'Nolan but 'when he chose to do so and pulled out his notebook Brian said: "I will have you know, Guard, that I am the man who wrote the road traffic regulations." "Well, indeed then, I am not a bit surprised," the guard replied wearily. "And you made a right hames of them, too." '

Early in the summer of 1988, as much in shame as anger, 'dear, dirty Dublin' seemed set to emerge as the greatest killjoy at its very own party. After ten centuries the city, which is fulcrum for one third of the Republic's 3.5 million people, appeared to have little spirit left for any Millennium celebrations. Urban squalor, the tyrannies of unemployment and drug crime had replaced much of its exuberant conviviality, and yet another generation of

15

well-educated, ambitious youngsters was escaping the dole queues by fleeing abroad. So what was left to cheer?

Dubliners pay some of the highest taxes in Europe while others in scarred Georgian slums bring a fetid realism to the imagery of Louis MacNeice who, years ago, foresaw Dublin's destiny as:

> *The bare bones of a fanlight*
> *over a hungry door.*

Just as in the case of Belfast, the normal process by which the past becomes harmless hasn't always happened in Dublin because in some quarters myth still contorts any real understanding of heroism. There is no easy answer to anything political on either side of the border because here are people whose ancient sufferings have made them skilled at hiding things both from the enemy and themselves. For all its sharp-tongued wit and bravado Dublin especially possesses an almost Eastern sense of camouflage, a verbal convolution intended to hold certain facts at bay. Even so, there are few cities which are as instantly engaging and humanly rewarding as Dublin with its salty air and pearly light, its garrulous boulevardiers and conspiratorial snugs, its serious bookshops and raffish browsers, its merciless sneer for those on high horses and its barmen, the best, some say, in the world, fast, vigilant but still decently unhurried in the matter of pouring pints. Against all expectations, though, the Millenium did force Dublin to rectify something of its double vision, a task carried on (although hindered by a derisory budget from the Government) in the 1991 designation of Dublin as European City of Culture. What first appeared as little more than a publicist's hype-fest emerged, for many, as another serious opportunity to examine in profound terms that complex tracery of charm and conflict, tease and back-bite which forms and plagues and energises the fabric of the city's life.

By beginning to rout out at least some of its urban disfigurement, the fight to regain Dublin's old elegance has taken a positive turn. One of the pleasures of a recent visit was the sight of rejuvenated Temple Bar, an artisans' neighbourhood only a stroll away from O'Connell Street. With its sympathetic industrial conversions, its artistic colony – the Project Arts Centre and the Irish Film Institute are here – and the beginnings of an ethnic restaurant culture, this compact but irregular stretch possesses something of the variegated interest found in the Marais in Paris before it became ultra-modish, a quality which still exists in the shrunken workers' quarters of New York's Lower East Side.

Along blustery reclaimed dockland Dublin is building an extensive international financial district to be flanked by sophisticated leisure facilities, but the prime aim of all such real estate is never the home market. That sleek, authoratitive bulk of the new Financial Services Centre rises like an enormous tanker on Custom House Docks. Its walls, gleaming with sea green glass, act as a metaphor for Dublin's new trading window on Europe and the world. With such conspicuous modernism at its elbow the Custom House itself has lost nothing of its splendour. In fact there is a heartening symbolism in the proximity, the old and the new of Dublin coming together in a manner that secures the distinctions of both. But if it were to possess no other architectural treasure than the Custom House, Dublin would still be worth a pilgrimage to see James Gandon's 18th century masterpiece. Viewed on a good day, from the DART platform at Tara Street Station, its classical symmetry and alabaster glow create a poetic kind of deportment, defying all those who claim that while Dublin may be handsome and Dublin may be grand, it is scarcely a capital beauty.

In 841 the Vikings founded a settlement which they called Dyflin, a corruption of the Gaelic Dubh Linn which means black pool. But it is as a city built in the colonial style of 18th century Britain that Dublin is mainly regarded, and there is an argument which insists that it has taken this length of time since the brutal fight for Independence for the 'glorious masonry of the overlords' to be respected by Dubliners themselves. In the case of Nelson's Pillar, however, the past proved a dogged obstacle to unambiguous affection. In 1966, 50 years after the Easter Rising, the IRA neatly blew the Admiral right off his fluted perch, leaving him as souvenir debris in the middle of O'Connell Street. But in reparation for all those early years of civic indifference the Royal Hospital at Kilmainham, one mile from the city centre, has been magnificently restored to act as National Centre for Culture and the Arts. Inspired by Les Invalides in Paris, it was built in 1680 by the Great Duke of Ormond and was designed by Sir William Robinson who later became the architect for Marsh's Library. Originally used as a home for old soldiers, it now provides a permanent site for the Irish Museum of Modern Art. Moving from there back towards the political hub of town, the former Royal College of Science displays the *grand luxe* confidence of Edwardian baroque. Today, after extensive refurbishment, it keeps a palatial roof over the Taoiseach's Office and regiments of civil servants.

But it is in its old vernacular architecture that Dublin really appeals. The householder's opulent use of colour, washing over brickwork and stone, shop front and door, could have been poured by some extravagant Latin impulse. Meany's newsagents stands on a corner of Blackrock, the yolky dazzle of its painted walls swimming into the eye of the beholder, like some gelataria on the Adriatic or a gypsy cave in Spain. Here and everywhere squat rows of cottages with brilliant doors display no reservations about nuzzling in beside those Georgian terraces of fanlight finesse and their own vivid entrances. There is a snugness about Dublin which no doubt turns the corner into claustrophobia and the nipped-back curtain of village snooping, but, on the whole, Dubliners ache from curiosity for the best of reasons. They are born gregarious, feeling no guilt at holding up the day's proceedings for the sake of a chat or a loaded riposte. 'What many strangers find difficult to comprehend,' says the politician Mary Harney, 'is that an appointment in Ireland is always a matter of approximate time and never intended to mean "on the dot".'

Fifty or 60 years ago when a woman's time contracted into labour in the Liberties her neighbours from those humble, comradely dwellings would cart her off to the Coombe maternity hospital with the loan of a nightdress and a promise to care for her other children as if they were their own. And if the newborn happened to be one of those 'premature' babes entering this vale of tears only four months after its mammy had been a bride, then the effortless ribaldry of sisterhood would despatch the explanation: 'Dear God, it must be indigestion from the wedding cake that brought it on.'

Dear God . . . Please God . . . Thank God . . . these little pledges of devotion still hang around Dublin conversation, sometimes as no more than a reflex of prayer-laden conditioning but more times as an echo of deep personal belief. The pulpit stridency of extreme Catholicism may be in retreat but in these modest pleadings and greetings to the deity Dublin and Ireland stand apart from much of Europe which has brazenly exchanged religion for commodities, yet still seeks the meditative havens of an interior life. Ireland's genuine spirituality is impressive, something remote from mawkish

incantations though those have often festooned the gabbled matins
of the sanctimonious. But at John Street Church, early on Saturday
morning, you see something of authentic prayer in the quiet devotions to Saint Rita of 50 or so people drawn together from all over
the city. You see it again when travelling south-bound on the DART
as a woman with eyes closed, and a violin case by her side, discreetly
plies the beads of a rosary tucked inside the pocket of her navy coat.
Close to the counter in that lovely old bar, the Long Hall at South
Great George's Street, Saint Anthony novena cards are propped next
to brochures for Clontarf Castle and coupons for a Jack Charlton
charity promotion called Score A Goal Against Poverty. By the
strength of its pastoral crusade for prayer the Church, in those early
years after Independence, helped the state to control any impatience
for material wealth among the people. They were long suffering
because it was the 'the will of God', a creed that today might well
help Mr Gorbachev, except that 75 years of totalitarian Com-
munism has effectively dismantled his people's faith in everything.

They say in Dublin, though, that had Jack Charlton stood in the
Irish Presidential election he would have ended up with his fishing
rods and football memorabilia installed in Aras an Uachtarain, the
President's official residence in Phoenix Park. No other English-
man – and a Protestant to boot – can have occupied such a proud
and loving place in Irish hearts. The rapture and good nature which
surrounded the Dublin homecoming of Jack's Lads after their
progression to the quarter-finals in 1990's World Cup marked not
only the delirious joy of the underdog triumphant but, on several
levels, it signalled a turning point in Irish self-esteem.

First, there was the exemplary bonhomie of the supporters,
Jack's Army, who shared, with Scotland, the honour of being
soccer's most lauded tourist soldiers in Italy. Secondly, there was
the team itself with its ebullient aerial bombardment which so
offended football purists but exhilarated the fans. And then there
were the players, many of whom were born in Britain, the children
and grandchildren of Irish emigrés now with speech thickened out
by scouse or tightened by that cockney edge. So, there it was again,
that word emigration, only now it wasn't just a branding of regret
and of dismal circumstances at home. No matter how temporarily,
a Geordie had turned the definition into something wonderful and
embracing, making the narrow mind of fundamental nationalism
seem very mean indeed.

Other parcels of history were handed out in the 12 months after Big Jack won his personal victory. Mary Robinson was given the people's vote as President, and Charles Haughey, never previously beheld as a visionary, stood up one day and astonished everyone by declaring he had a dream. Change, choice and contradiction, indeed. But hold on . . . Dublin's true annus mirabilis is still around the corner.

2

CITY, STATE AND CHURCH
Mary Robinson

IT WAS IN Ballinamuck that the first spectre of failure emerged for Fianna Fail. When the Presidential ballot box was opened there on a bright November morning in 1990 Mary Robinson was discovered to be only nine votes behind Brian Lenihan's 109. The little town of pigs in County Longford might not have toppled the Old Guard completely but it had shaken a fierce fist at it and after more than 50 years of solid conformity Ballinamuck had told Fianna Fail not to presume on its goodwill any longer.

For the Irish psyche the impact of Mary Robinson's triumph was almost the equivalent of the Berlin Wall's collapse. The Republic's electorate had voted not just to put a formidable barrister and a woman into the Park – a reference to the President's official Dublin mansion in Phoenix Park – but to accentuate that historic moment by selecting a woman whose determined liberal principles threatened the country's wealthiest and most muscular establishment. And although her victory might have been masterminded in Dublin, it could not have been achieved had her message struck a wrong note with rural communities, some of them perched on the very periphery of Western Europe. Of course, the President, born in County Mayo, is a Westerner herself but that doesn't entirely explain this electoral distinction. Dick Walsh, political editor of the *Irish Times*, provides a more profoundly reassuring assessment. In his opinion Mary Robinson's campaigners avoided not only the usual left-wing mistake of limiting a candidate's appeal to those

fitting a very narrow definition of working class but also 'the notion prevalent in sections of Fine Gael and most of Fianna Fail that concern for ethics or social justice or modernisation is confined to a single postal district in Dublin where no real Irish person ever lived'.

Mary Robinson is 48 now and one of those individuals whose forcefulness in public debate contrasts with a natural shyness and reserve. In 1970 she married Nick Robinson, a Protestant and a Dublin law academic who is also widely known as a cartoonist. They have three children, Tessa, William and Aubrey. 'Even if she had lost the election I'd say the campaign was good for Mary,' reflected her husband. 'It brought her out of her shell.' But long before that she had not always been a vision of gravitas. At university Mary Robinson was an active member of the drama society, and a close friend recalls that, many years ago, she turned up at a party so convincingly disguised as a gum-chewing American tourist in a platinum wig that the hostess never detected her real identity.

Although the Presidency of Ireland is mainly a ceremonial role it is Mrs Robinson's intention to give its symbolism dynamic and democratic relevance. 'Citizens of Ireland,' she began her inaugural address, 'you have chosen me to represent you and I am humbled by and grateful for your trust.' Symbols, she said, can be potent, determining the kind of history we make and remake. Essentially President Robinson represents the new self-confident face of Irish womanhood. Dublin today teems with gifted women working in key posts in most of the professions and the arts, and their very presence there signifies an old, isolated culture moving through all manner of growing pains to find a modern place amid the tumult of Europe.

The Presidential election was never intended as a political event but it became precisely that because of the Lenihan Tapes. This fiasco, hailed with some relish by pub philosophers as Dublingate, erupted during the last ten days of the campaign and, for reasons of political expediency, led to Brian Lenihan's sacking from the Cabinet posts of Tanaiste (deputy Prime Minister) and Minister for Defence. At the heart of the row was the accusation that Mr Lenihan had lied and counter-lied in interviews concerning an attempt to pressure President Hillery into making Charles Haughey an unelected Taoiseach in 1982. Here was exposed yet another instance of Fianna Fail's old cocky assumption that it alone had the divine right to govern. But if the Presidential election proved anything it was that the conservtive consensus in Ireland is crumbling; that people no longer wish to be represented only by rigid cultural structures which prevent them from breaking loose of the past.

Mary Robinson, an Independent but backed by both the Labour and Workers Parties during the Presidential campaign, has always stood for a pluralist society where the human rights of everyone, from the illegitimate to those seeking divorce, must be respected. All those bogeymen words, which in the past had worked in Fianna Fail's favour, failed on this occasion. The slurs that a vote for President Robinson would put 'a commie in the Park', or turn the official residence, Aras An Uachtarain, into an abortion referral clinic, were easily detected by the electorate as the desperate tactics of a party on the run.

As the final votes indicated, a significant section of society – the majority of whom are below the age of 45 – would have none of it. Although she did not top the poll when all the first preference votes were counted Mary Robinson was assured of victory because of her pact to exchange second preferences with the third Presidential candidate, Fine Gael's Austin Currie.

The 'commie' smear was among the most ridiculous. Even by today's Gucci standards, President Robinson would never pass muster as a Red. She is the only daughter among five children of a middle-class family from Mayo's Ballina. Her father, Dr Aubrey Bourke, a patrician figure in his mid-seventies, still lives in the town and during the Twenties he studied medicine at Edinburgh University where an uncle was a medical Fellow. Many of her late mother's relatives have Edinburgh and Glasgow connections.

From that moment in April 1990 when Mary Robinson chose to declare her candidacy for the highest office in Ireland the very nature of the Presidential election was bound to change. For the first time a woman was challenging the established order of state affairs in a country where worship for the Madonna is fervent but the erosion of women's dignity is not uncommon. So the issue became much more than the selection of a figurehead who could take a decent salute. The vote represented a choice between two Irelands: the old and the new, the compulsively secret wheeler-dealery of atavistic patriotism, and the vision of a future Ireland freed of corroded enmities and political slyness in a determination to be open, inclusive and tolerant.

A clever and amiable man, Brian Lenihan has always been held in great affection throughout his 30 years in politics. But it is scarcely two years since he underwent drastic surgery for a liver transplant and, although the operation has been exceptionally successful, others always worried that his health might become impaired had he won the Presidency with its unremitting rounds of social engagements. Lenihan himself always dismissed this concern as nonsensical fuss, insisting that if the cut and thrust of political life had caused him no bad post-operative effects then certainly the fine bone china ambience of Aras an Uachtarain wasn't likely to impose too much tyrannical strain. Given the eventual outcome of the Presidential election, in which Mr Lenihan was left bereft of ministerial kudos, those words are poignant indeed. Fianna Fail, the richest yet most classless political party in the Republic, still regard themselves as de Valera's Soldiers of Destiny and thus the heirs to unfettered control of power throughout the country. But times change, if not the zeal of political mullahs, and Taoiseach Charles Haughey's failure to win a handle on the Presidency raised doubts about his leadership of the party on two levels. First he had sacrificed his 'old friend' to no avail. (In the light of the furore Haughey had dismissed Lenihan so as to avert a vote of no confidence in the Irish Parliament, the Dail. However, only hours before he had declared he had in no way demanded his deputy's resignation.) Secondly, Charles Haughey is now more than ever synonymous with the art of cronyism, a political order of privilege and favours which may have served Ireland relatively well in past generations but which today is increasingly perceived as doomed. Even so Haughey himself remains one of the wiliest politicians in Europe, a political Lazarus ever capable of rising from the dead, and it is this reputation plus his certain *magnifico* lifestyle which earns him the gruff admiration of many and persuades others that he is still far from receiving a terminal blow.

Yet if Fianna Fail ended up in disarray so too did Fine Gael whose own Presidential candidate was Austin Currie, formerly from Dungannon in County Tyrone and now resident in Dublin. Although he personally conducted an honourable campaign, Currie was blighted mainly by general public dissatisfaction with the then leader of his party, Alan Dukes, a civilised and scholarly politician but with no grassroots rapport.

However, the campaign also exposed one of Ireland's uglier

national traits. If there were those who smeared Mary Robinson for being a woman there were others (and perhaps they were the same people) who felt compelled to brand Currie as an impudent outsider who had no right to contemplate office in the South. The symmetry of such crude prejudice was inescapable for here was the same kind of bigotry, voiced in a different accent, that had smeared and challenged his heroism as an SDLP politician with John Hume in the North. In fact only one established political leader emerged from the Presidential race with increased credit and that was Labour's Dick Spring whose astute legal mind, in recent years, has been quick to expose unconstitutional tactics by Fianna Fail, and who, still in his forties, belongs to that age group which is raising public consciousness in areas of international debate.

Mary Robinson belongs to that generation too. At the age of 25 she was the youngest professor of law to be appointed to Trinity College in Dublin, and for 20 years she was a member of the Senate where she began spectacularly enough by raising the question of access to contraception. With others she worked to establish the right of women to participate in jury duty, and on the provision of legal aid in family law cases. She campaigned for separate taxation for the sexes, for equality to be enshrined within the social welfare code and, although she has long been an active crusader for Cherish, which supports single parents, she has also courageously defended the rights of students to receive information about abortion. At the Dublin Well Women Clinic the staff's affection for her is irrepressible and the same strong bond of emotion is apparent at Cherish, where she has been president since 1973. Instrumental in ensuring that illegitimacy no longer carries legal penalities, Mary Robinson has also continually been a brave, sure voice on the rights of travelling people, and, in a celebrated case six years ago, she acted successfully for journalists whose phones were illegally tapped by the authorities. Her resignation from the Labour Party was characteristically principled: a protest against the imposition of the Anglo-Irish Agreement on the Unionist community who had not been consulted about its terms.

Throughout her adult life, then, Mary Robinson has been no stranger to conservative ire and although she describes the Presidency as 'a modest office' her tenure for the remaining six years is likely to bring discomfort to Irish fundamentalists. But already her wish that Article 1 of the Agreement (guaranteeing the right of the people of Northern Ireland to self-determination) be included in the Republic's Constitution has initiated positive discussion, and at her urging there is also growing acknowledgment among a younger electorate that Articles 2 and 3 of that Constitution are today both offensive and anachronistic in their claim that the re-integration of the North is the Irish Republic's national imperative.

Of course there are those who argue that Mary Robinson's elevation to symbolic head of state is a grievous loss to the fraught arena of social reform in Ireland, for here is a formidable campaigner now locked within the straitjacket of protocol, a woman who is far too bright to be content with the smiling chit-chat and leafy isolation of Pheonix Park. Yet anyone who knows Mary Robinson well is convinced that, despite all the constraints, she can develop the role in a manner which consolidates the call for transformed attitudes in Ireland. After all with words alone she has possibly done more than any single politician to induce change in a country which has steadfastly set its face against reform.

Even so, as the Dublin journalist Geraldine Kennedy has observed, President Robinson will have to pursue 'a prudent course if she doesn't want to appear to be a frenzied social worker, or running the country'. But Dick Walsh, of the *Irish Times*, believes that the Robinson campaign was not merely about making her the President. Instead ' it asked us to make a statement about ourselves and in particular about the issues she so clearly raised: the march of women towards full citizenship which is still denied them; the conditions of the poor whose poverty is even now denied; and the shabby habit of closing doors – on the backs of emigrants, on the hopes of the young, on the rights of minorities'.

If Ireland is not yet on the threshold of these achievements, Walsh insists that it is for those still in the thick of the political fight to ensure the momentum generated by the President is not lost. 'In a sense the people voted confidence in each other and in their community's generosity of spirit.' And their decision stands in splendid contrast to that amalgam of greed, begrudgery and meanness which has come to be called the National Sleaze.

For the Dublin poet Paul Durcan, Mary Robinson's election was this century's last chance for a candle to be lit in modern Ireland. 'Had she failed the forces of darkness would have won, telling us something terrible about ourselves. It would have confirmed our inability or refusal to grow up and turn away from civil war politics.' Twelve months on, having the right woman in the Park is not only gradually cutting Ireland's infamous male braggarts down to size but doing much for a small country's overseas esteem. And 12 November 1990 has now been enshrined in the calendar of nationhood, for in the same week that Berlin celebrated the first week of its demolished Wall, the Irish Republic strode proudly out of backwoods politics.

3

SCENES
The Strange Case of the Virgin Condom

BY LUNCHTIME talk in the basement bar at Buswell's Hotel in Dublin is swerving towards the imperative: 'Tell me this,' says one politician to another. 'Are we the only country in the western world where the entire nature of democracy rests on the availability of a packet of condoms?' The second politician stares intently at his glass of stout: 'I'd say we are. Not even Italy, with the Pope living round the corner, landed itself with this one.' There was a point in 1991 when the ramifications of the row caused by the Government's decision to amend the Republic's limited laws on contraception threatened to engulf every aspect of conversation in the capital. While the hierarchy ranted, an increasingly secular flock used the letter columns of newspapers to challenge the Church for playing the 'Catholic card' on the issue. Significantly the *Irish Times* received more correspondence on condoms than it did on the matter of how best to commemorate the 75th anniversary of the Easter Rising.

So, what was it all about? To begin almost at the beginning . . . Early in 1991 Richard Branson appeared in Dublin's District Court in an unlikely alliance with the Irish Family Planning Association. At least that is how it might have seemed to anyone not versed in that short, drab work, *The History of Sex in Ireland*. Anyway, Branson was there because the IFPA had been caught selling condoms from a stall in his Virgin Megastore on Aston Quay. This facility, which contravened Ireland's rudimentary laws on birth control, began in 1988, drawing at least 100 customers a week. The first case against the IFPA for such commercial activity was dismissed on a technicality but at the end of the second case the association was fined £370, a crippling sum given its threadbare resources. Which is why it was back in court that Thursday, appealing against conviction. It was the feast of St Valentine and the irony seemed tailor-made.

Some weeks later judgment was passed, increasing the fine to £500, and in reference to that sum Dublin's Circuit Court judge, Sean D. O'Hanrahan, claimed that the association had 'got off lightly'. No further appeal was available but the decision triggered an angry reaction of incredulity and political stramash. Describing the 1985 Family Planning Act as 'unsatisfactory and outdated', the Taoiseach, Charles Haughey, in a rare expression of social angst, promised legislation which would be more in line with modern realities. The existing provision limited the sale of birth control products to chemists, health boards and a restricted number of other outlets. But new proposals, urged on by the Taoiseach in the fight against AIDS, sought to make condoms more widely obtainable, without prescription, to people from the age of 16. Within days, however, the fog of 'further discussions' was already blurring any enlightenment. 'Wait till we go to Mass,' mused one Fianna Fail member. 'Then we'll see the croziers flying in every direction.'

Mr Haughey insisted, however, that despite the 'shock' and 'nausea' which his 'misconceived' proposals had inflicted on the clergy, the final decision would be the Government's alone: 'Taken by the Government, as the Government, and thereafter it will be Government policy . . .' Ultimately, however, the issue was subject to compromise, condemned by many as a 'cop-out'. The Government reduced the age limit for condom purchase to 17, not 16, permitting their sale only from outlets found suitable and registered by health boards. Thus mobile outlets, street traders and – most significantly – vending machines would be excluded.

Inevitably there were some reservations about Branson's involvement. The master balloonist and entrepreneurial adventurer is a tycoon much skilled in the craft of public relations. But the legal risks of his Virgin involvement with the IFPA were always understood (he in fact paid the association's fine). And in effect the case became a national crusade against Ireland's pitiful family planning services and the dangerous indifference which has always surrounded Government policy on AIDS. In the Republic, the incidence of AIDS is now doubling every 16 months, mostly through drug abuse and prostitution. Yet although this rate is considerably higher than the European average there is scarcely any co-ordinated education programme and no substantially funded system of caring for victims with dignity and compassion. Like many concerned people in Dublin Branson has spoken out about this shameful indifference: 'Condoms are the principal weapon in the fight to stop the spread of AIDS,' he told the District Court. Previously he had informed journalists that he found it incredible that at a time when most countries were spending huge sums to persuade young people to use condoms, attempts were being made in Ireland to prevent them.

Up to this point Fianna Fail's sluggish response suggested a contempt for such urgent views. Twelve months previously, when Mr Haughey was enjoying Dublin's presidency of the European Community, a special EC team monitoring AIDS was meeting in the capital, advocating increased expenditure to stave off further epidemic. This was on the very same day that the District Court imposed its fine on the IFPA. For its part the IFPA struggled on, ensnared by the most restrictive code of practice in Western Europe. According to the previous law, contraceptives were only available to married couples through chemists and a few other limited outlets. However, those chemists who are conscientious objectors to 'the immorality of prophylactic rubber' are not obliged to stock condoms. In relation to the new law the question is now being raised in the Dail as to whether those barmen who may also be conscientious objectors will be safeguarded in their jobs should they refuse to sell condoms with a pint.

Because of embarrassment and Ireland's aptitude for guilt-ridden conditioning, there are plenty of people who have preferred to make such personal purchases down among the rock numbers at Virgin. Interestingly, the IFPA's research indicates that 90 per cent of those buying condoms there are men, mostly below the age of 25. Sales increase notably before holiday weekends and rugby internationals, and there is a considerable trade with young couples up in Dublin from the country. Predictably, Catholic revisionists have been swift to denounce this information as evidence that, thanks to pagan outside influences, the country is going to the devil. But time is running out for the old guard. As expressed on phone-in radio programmes and in newspaper correspondence, the views of the people suggest that the hierarchy and inflexible Fianna Fail parliamentarians are out of touch with public opinion on the subject. Indeed Ireland has recently elected a President who began her days in the Senate on this very issue of access to birth control.

That was 20 years ago and it has taken this long for a generation to emerge which openly shuns the duplicity of solving unwanted pregnancies with clandestine abortions in Britain. If nothing else the IFPA survey reveals young people's greater sense of responsibility about sex. And among the more liberal clergy there is a realisation now that anyone seeking to roll back the timid steps taken towards cultural pluralism is finally on a loser, especially as such action would be seen as an attack on a better status for women in Irish society. 'The jig is up in that respect,' says one priest. 'A Catholic Church which tells its faithful that birth control is a sin cannot hope to survive in the context of 1991. It just can't.'

In the Seventies that cultivated Irish senator, Alexis FitzGerald Sr, said as much during a debate on the subject when he confessed he was *past* it but *for* it. And with characteristic *brio* an actress reflects that as long ago as 1979, during the papal visit to Ireland: 'Diaphragms were flying out the windows, like frisbees, all over residential Dublin.' A week later, after the spiritual high was over and the Pope had returned happily to Rome, the city was back to its old ways, upholding the faith with a nudge and a wink, and a pocket filled with contraband contraceptives. To all but Catholic fundamentalists the modest alteration to the old law represents a sensible precaution, but suddenly the rhetoric of the Dark Ages began to thunder around the country as the hierarchy and certain hellfire politicians orchestrated their outrage. 'I lived for years on the Continent and witnessed the degrading display of these objects,' fumed the Rev. Dr Vincent Twomey, a lecturer in moral theology, referring to the sale of condoms. 'Is this the kind of Europe we want to emulate?'

The Bishop of Limerick, Dr Jeremiah Newman, condemned the linkage between AIDS prevention and condoms as 'a red herring of the first order', while the Archbishop of Dublin, Dr Desmond Connell, found it 'extraordinary that no political party in the country is prepared to defend what so many people regard as fundamental values of family life'. But the core of Dr Connell's complaint is surely that there is no longer a political party in Ireland which is prepared to do the Church's bidding. Nonetheless, there are enough recalcitrant politicians in Fianna Fail particularly to derail Mr Haughey's improbable Pauline conversion to social change. He has, after all, already had to amend his original desire to lower the age for contraceptive use to 16, even though this is the age when couples may marry.

And that vision of a pluralist society articulated by President Robinson in her inaugural speech in November 1990 has so far received scant endorsement from Ireland's spiritual leader, the Archbishop of Armagh and Primate of All Ireland, Cardinal Cahal Daly. He remains a fastidious custodian of Catholicism's opposition to birth control, divorce and homosexuality, but as a result of a ruling from the European Court of Human Rights a law to legalise this last practice is now on the Irish agenda. However, maybe to avoid further collision between the Church and secular life, the expected White Paper on marital breakdown studiously avoids the actual word, divorce.

If any man knows how the orthodox Church might exploit fractured marriages to its advantage it is Mr Haughey. In the 1980s, as Opposition leader, he and traditionalist clerics formed a militant alliance which thoroughly destroyed Garret FitzGerald's valiant attempts to reform the Constitution with referenda on abortion and divorce. Today, though, we see a reborn Taoiseach, shaken by the Robinson Presidential victory but now forced to concede that Fianna Fail's only route to survival lies in being the architect of 'a new caring society that belongs among the advanced nations of Europe'. Yet it may require gale-force winds to loosen entrenched prejudice in Ireland for the findings of a recent study from the university at Maynooth reveal many people to be distressingly intolerant of other religious faiths. According to sociologist the Rev. Dr Micheal MacGreil, 51 per cent of those interviewed would not marry or welcome a Methodist into their families; 60 per cent would not welcome or marry a Jew; 69 per cent would not marry an agnostic, and 71 per cent would baulk at the very thought of an atheist.

These disclosures speak volumes about the pinched mentality of provincialism, and the uncomprehending bigotry that results from a single Church insisting that its teaching carries the force of law, applicable not only to its own believers but those who live by other rules. If, as the politician Alan Dukes has observed, Ireland seems more tolerant today, that may be because of a growing secular awareness rather than any active concern with religious liberty. So could the brave and visionary be penalised for pursuing an open, inclusive society? Those politicians in Buswell's across from the seat of Parliament, the Dail, might still have got it precisely right. The furore wasn't just another fight about contraception but an exploration of the type of democracy people want for modern Ireland. Yet, what exceptional poetic justice it would have been had Mr Haughey, of all men, been felled as well as foiled by the Case of the Virgin Condom.

VIEWS FROM CORRESPONDENTS
Some extracts from letters in the *Irish Times*:

Sir, – The Hierarchy are all up in their high hats about the dreaded 'C' word and are obviously very worried about what the politicians, if left to their own devices, might do. I hope that they might be as worried about, and would try to educate, the upwards of 39 per cent of their flock who would refuse citizenship to Hari Krishnas, Muslims and even Jews, not to mention the seven per cent who would actually deport any atheists they got their hand on. (Figures from the Rev. MacGreil's recent survey of religious practice in Ireland.)

Blackrock, 18 March 1991.

Sir, – . . . I also note that the issues of unwanted children, abortions, compulsory weddings and the frequently related separations or beatings, sexually transmitted diseases, premature ageing of women and poverty through overbreeding and a host of other problems do not figure in the anti-condom arguments. A narrow morality indeed.

Naas, 21 March 1991.

Sir, – As it would appear that our Republic is managed by both the Government and the Hierarchy would it be correct to describe it as a condominium which my dictionary (Collins) defines as meaning 'joint rule or sovereignty'?

Drogheda, 5 April 1991.

Sir, – It's great that the youth of Ireland have absolutely nothing to worry about. If they use condoms they won't get AIDS. If they don't use condoms and they get AIDS at least they'll go straight to heaven.

Sutton, 26 March, 1991.

THE STRANGE CASE OF THE VIRGIN CONDOM

Sir, – I refer to your Dail report of March 13th in which Deputy Pat McCartan asked Dr O'Hanlon to ensure that 'no belt of a crozier from any quarter will dictate to the Government or to the House on what was clearly a health matter . . .' Surely this is unparliamentary language. Deputy McCartan is perfectly entitled to express his views on episcopal intervention or interference by the hierarchy. Let us hope that the Committee on Procedure and Privilege will encourage deputies to refrain from using language not befitting ladies – or gentlemen. Courtesy costs nothing.

Ranelagh, 26 March 1991.

Following the announcement by the Taoiseach of the proposed reduction in the age limit for the purchase of condoms and an increase in their availability, Bishop Newman is reported as saying that such a change was as 'misconceived as it was shocking'. Surely he could not be further from the truth? The benefits of the proposed changes being the prevention of shock, through the promotion of misconception.

Terenure, 26 March 1991.

4

VOICES
Dermot Bolger

DERMOT BOLGER has never attempted to camouflage his subversive desire. 'I wanted to take the Irish literary novel and kill it,' he says. *The Journey Home* provided him with the means for such merciless disposal. By applying a flint-edged lyricism to violent hunger, Bolger made the squalid needlework of heroin addiction seem all the more terrible. But beyond that, his third novel exposes the sour poisons of governmental neglect. Almost surgically he lays bare the foul housing and decrepit lives of Dublin, its sly racketeers and easy abandonment of no-hopers where poverty hardens over everything like a scab.

Bolger, both playwright and novelist, was born in 1959 in what was the Finglas wasteland of North Dublin, an urban development of Romanian grimness with no services. His sardonically affectionate play, *The Lament for Arthur Cleary*, was premiered at the Dublin Theatre Festival in 1989 and later won the Samuel Beckett Award for a Best Performed First Play. It was also received with acclaim at the Edinburgh Festival and at the Riverside Studios in Hammersmith, London, during an impressive Irish Arts Festival in 1990. 'Arthur Cleary is really a portrait of Dublin in the mid-eighties,' says Bolger. At that time the city's drug problem had reached grievous proportions while rampant materialism turned greed into a moral crusade. 'Arthur returns to the city to discover it has changed beyond all recognition.' The play's theme is inspired by an ancient Irish poem, *The Lament of Art O'Leary*, in which

37

a nobleman comes back to Ireland from foreign parts to learn that it has been radically altered by the penal laws. 'He refuses to comply and is killed for his pains. On finding him dead, his wife, being a good Gaelic woman, composes a 7,000-word lament on the spot.'

Since Bolger abhors artists who merely serve tradition, what is he doing exploiting past literature in this way? He is, however, well able to defend his nod in the direction of Art O'Leary. He sees it not as a continuation of tradition, but more a rummage through it 'to carry away something that suits me'. Artistically *The Journey Home* may be an uneven book but it burns with justifiable and reassuring anger. Dermot Bolger, still living in Dublin's north-side, knows his territory with its thickets of scummy corruption and collapse, its small respectable citizens struggling against the bully's shove and gaunt despair. 'People have said that book depicts hidden Dublin but it is the only Dublin I have ever known. Growing up on that side of a dual carriageway, playing soccer on the same piece of ground where the Finglas people keep their horses.'

With his wife and small son, Bolger lives in one of Drumcondra's pleasing little red-brick houses, not far from the room above an off-licence shop in which he operates the Raven Arts Press, his one-man publishing venture to promote the more iconoclastic of Ireland's young writers.

Dublin, he says, is a very special city, yet it is like others the world over in the sense that it shares the same urban problems. 'Even so Dublin is different in that parts of it remain very rural. Still, if you go back to rural Ireland these days that can also be disorientating because you can find a man in tweeds with a clay pipe, and a satellite dish in the haggard behind him.'

As for Bolger himself, he remains that most intricately partisan of Dubliners, eternally critical of the city's betrayals but a smitten defender to the end. His thoughts are worth quoting at length: 'One of my plays, *The Holy Ground*, is about a woman whose husband is a chauvinist brute, completely off the wall. He hasn't spoken to her for 25 years and she leads a sort of subterranean life hunched up in the living room, watching the television with the sound turned down while every politician in the land works overtime to gain her husband's vote. At 60 years of age she realises that her whole life is wasted and she actually puts rat poison in his dinner but the joke is that the rat poison doesn't work. He has thrombosis and the rat poison contains warfarin which is an ingredient for thinning out the blood. So all she really does is keep this monstrous man alive. But at the play's Dublin preview at the Gate Theatre, there was a row of women – the youngest was about 50 and the eldest I'd say was about 70 with a beret on her head. This group just loved it. Every one of those women wanted to take a pickaxe to the man and smash him to pieces. Those women, most of whom must have married around the same time as the character in the play, were, by their enjoyment, really challenging society for the roles it had imposed on them. They were open-minded and questioning in a way that would have been unthinkable ten years ago. At the Gate this play ran in a double bill with *In High Germany*, another play of mine about a guy who takes to the bed, shuts himself away from the world but the world feels he should be saved and the busybodies arrive to do just that: first the Mormons, followed by the Church, then the drug squad and the Government. There were irreverent references in it but once again the older Dublin women in the audience loved it; they were breaking their hearts laughing at it. However, when the Peacock presented *Blinded by the Light*, there were a few walk-outs, and every time it was the same type of person: a 42-year-old businessman and his wife. They didn't mind me slagging off their God but they weren't going to see their building society ridiculed. In fact the very people you would have thought were liberal sophisticates were very pissed off by it altogether while the old people loved it.

'There are different levels of corruption in Ireland and up to now people have kept quiet about it or else made a joke of it because in the end the corruption didn't seem so terrible, and anyway people here like crooks so long as they aren't murderous thugs.

'The Irish, in fact, have a great anarchic streak, a disrespect for authority which in many ways is good. And this goes right to the top. Hence the Brian Lenihan story about the time when he was Minister for Education and on those days when nothing much was doing he'd take off to one of his favourite pubs in Kilcock, just outside Dublin. This particular day he asks the secretary if there was anything important scheduled and the secretary says no and after a few hours the wretched secretary realises there is indeed a sudden meeting that he hasn't told your man about so he frantically rings the place in Kilcock. When the phone is picked up he asks: "Is that so and so's shop?" and a voice replies: "Yes." Then he asks: "Is there a bar in the back?" The voice replies: "Yes." So the secretary asks: "Is Brian Lenihan there?" And the voice replies: "Speaking." The Minister had actually answered the phone. Now that's a great story and on one level the whole country loves Brian Lenihan for it. But at the same time people now ask: "What the hell was the Minister of Education, earning X number of thousands of pounds, doing at a pub in the middle of the afternoon?"

'Fianna Fail works on the basis that there is no class; that we're all republicans, and that's a very persuasive argument. It isn't true, of course, but it's persuasive and it lures people into believing that we're all the same. But Fianna Fail is unique in that it has always attracted both the very rich and the very poor, unusual for what was once a radical party. It is the party of business at the same time as being the party of working class people like my father, a sailor for 42 years of his life. But he would never vote Labour. Labour in his day was beyond the pale, and as for Fine Gael that was for rich professionals.

'Yet prior to independence there was a labour movement here and Ireland was considered very radical. We had Countess Markievicz, a workers' militant and the first woman to win a seat at Westminster, although she never attended, and we had A.E., George Russell.

'And in 1913, when Lenin rallied forth the workers of Europe to rise to his revolution, the only place that rose was Limerick. The city of Limerick formed a soviet which was put down by the British Army, the IRA and the Church. Obviously nobody wanted a soviet Limerick. But always the Labour Party was prevailed upon, in the national interest, to step aside until the national question was resolved. In effect Fianna Fail and Fine Gael have used the North of Ireland, rather in the way that the Americans have used the Russians, as the bogeyman. They have exploited the northern situation to control their own people so that they would never ask for change at home. By saying that when we get a united country we'll be able to solve all other problems they have blamed the North for their own inadequacies, telling us that all the woes we were suffering from came from being a divided island aching from a phantom pain.

'This is the old, rhetorical unfinished story that goes on and on and on and holds up everything. It is what the Brian Lenihans of the world have always stood for, whereas Mary Robinson stands for saying the North may be something we cannot solve at this very moment, but let us solve the things that can be solved, the concrete, practical everyday things. And this isn't just a Dublin thing. My favourite piece of news during the Presidential election was that when Ballinamuck – not the most cosmopolitan place in the world – opened the ballot box there were 100 votes for Mary Robinson and 109 for Brian Lenihan. Now all right, if that had been an election for Taoiseach then Lenihan would have walked home because the majority of Ireland still wouldn't want a radical left politician running the country, but what people have said by voting Robinson in as President is that yes, new Ireland should have a voice that can be heard. Having a different viewpoint in the Park has made people feel good. It's a psychic shock to the establishment, not a political one. We can say we have a woman President with a radical outlook and that makes us feel we are taking the steps towards becoming a modern country.

'I believe that people are taking themselves more seriously and two particular things are giving us a sense of pride. The first is football and the success of the World Cup team. During the competition a TV presenter was congratulating Mick McCarthy and saying that even if the team got no further it would have done marvellously well. But McCarthy's attitude was a tremendous rejection of the old Irish habit of settling for second best. He said: "But we don't like being beaten by anybody." There is a brilliant biography of the patriot Padraig Pearse, *The Triumph of Failure*, in which the author Ruth Dudley Edwards argues that Pearse sets out to lose the Easter Rising knowing that loss will win him a place in history as a vindicator. The Irish football team completely discredited that kind of attitude and when the team returned, a huge crowd gathered to cheer them and there wasn't a single arrest. Just pride and friendship and great good humour to welcome the lads back to Dublin. But when the Lord Mayor came out to stand with the team, the crowd booed because the Lord Mayor was Charlie Haughey's son. To get the crowd to shut up Jack Charlton put his arm around him and sure enough the crowd shut up. They went quiet but only for Jack.

'The second thing that is having a sobering effect on Irish people today is emigration. When Brian Lenihan sought to excuse emigration by saying, "We can't all live on this small island," it was a brilliant cop-out, a politician blaming the size of the country for government mismanagement, and the people saw it as such. Our

41

young people now are some of the best educated in Europe and when they go abroad for work they are to Ireland what champagne is to France: they travel well. But people question more deeply now why Ireland must continually be the home you leave.

'As for Dublin writers, there was a generation in the Fifties and Sixties that wrote one book and sat on it and never wrote another. "I'm a writer," was the introduction you heard in every Dublin pub. But today young Irish writers are delivering the goods, writing novels, plays and poetry and not sitting, swilling the talent away in pubs. All right we may get slagged in every Dublin pub as the Ballygowan generation, sipping mineral water, but we're doing the business. We're not pissed out of our brains in the way that outsiders expect every Irish writer to be. Ten years ago when I started the Raven Arts Press to promote the prose and poetry of new writers I admired, I very quickly encountered rigid notions of what Irish writing was supposed to be about. I remember a British publisher telling me: "When I want to read about urban blight I read a poet from Hull. When I want to read about cows I read a poet from Ireland." It was like an EC poetry quota. Irish poetry had to work to the quota.

'Today when I go to a reception I dress like a Bulgarian trade diplomat, in a suit and tie. But you still meet critics, journalists and broadcasters, English mostly, who want you to have had seven pints of Guinness by two o' clock in the afternoon. That's all gone. People, not just artists, are going for success spurred on by others like U2, Jack Charlton's army, Mary Robinson and Seamus Heaney and theatre/film directors like Jim Sheridan and the producer Noel Pearson. This is what the new nationalism is about – a healthy self-respect.

'But when I was growing up in the Seventies there were two Irelands. There was the official Ireland refusing to legislate for the real Ireland. So you had the whole clandestine thing of breaking the law in order to get contraceptives, sneaking them for those occasions when you thought you might need them . . . and, of course, you never did. What keeps me here in Dublin is that I love it. I have always refused to leave. It was a deliberate cultural decision. I didn't want to view Ireland, like so many, from the safe distance of Paris. And I like the attitude of the people. I feel at home here. I take my dog for a walk in the park at night and I may meet an old man of 80, a complete stranger but we can talk to one another and have a few laughs. I doubt if that would happen so readily in England or Germany. There is great tolerance and good humour here. In Finglas, in North Dublin, a place dropped in the middle of nowhere with no services, no nothing, ordinary working-class people keep horses on the green. Those on the South Side of the city with horse boxes think it's disgraceful, of course, but the Finglas horses are very well cared for and loved. But outsiders reinforce the stereotypes about the poorer areas of the city. One of my books was set in Finglas and absolutely every critic mentioned joy-riders in their reviews yet there wasn't a single joy-rider in the plot. But although Dublin does give me a sense of belonging I don't particularly enjoy being in the public eye – fame is too big a word for it. Writing has made me a few shillings and brought me some awards but I keep away from the parties and receptions when I can. My favourite story about writers and fame concerns an old guy called Charlie who used to be in a factory where I once worked. Decades ago Charlie was a messenger boy and one day when he was sent into town he saw Yeats walking through the streets, waving his hands in the air and he said to someone: "Who's yer man? Is he a lunatic or what?" And the other person says: "Ah no, that's Willie Yeats. He's a poet, like, and he always goes on like that." So some weeks later Charlie is sent to Yeats's home to deliver a parcel and Yeats answers the door and Charlie says :"Ah, Jasus, I hear you're a great man for the old pomes . . ." And Yeats asks: "Who told you that?" and Charlie replies: "Some fella told me that." So Yeats brought him in and Charlie recites word for word for Yeats the entire first act of *Julius Caesar* that he'd learned at school. And Yeats gave him cake and lemonade and chewed the cud for two hours before packing him off. It's a lovely story but it's the only one where Yeats comes across as a likeable person, a warm human being.

'Dublin allows you to be yourself and it is a city that leaves you alone, if that is what you wish. But it is a very literate place with a tremendous number of news periodicals and magazines for its size. And I believe that if you were to stop and ask people in the street to name you half a dozen Irish writers they could do it and I guarantee you the writers wouldn't all be dead ones. Ask them the same question in London and they'd be flummoxed.'

5

CITY, STATE AND CHURCH
Dublin's Unfair City

MORE THAN MANY Western countries, the Irish Republic is
being urged to confront the most elusive aspects of its nature and
rectify sins of omission. Inevitably it is an intense, and often
agonising exercise, veering from a painful revision of de Valera's
stifling, idealised nationalism with its rigid obedience to Rome to
the woeful hilarity of the Virgin Condom episode where much bitter
wit surrounded the realisation that Ireland in 1991 was perhaps the
only country in the world requiring Government legislation for the
sale of rubber prophylactics. But the fact that profound reassess-
ment is taking place in some of Dublin's most influential quarters
indicates not just an expedient desire to conform to outside
demands. It represents, after 70 years of independence, a mature
surge for change from within the country, a deep wish on the part
of a young nation to exorcise the ghosts of tortured history and
establish a small but distinctive place within Mr Gorbachev's dream
of a common European home. Ireland, then, is being asked, both
by itself and others, to move forward from an atavistic nationalist
credo to embrace political, social and economic pluralism. With
much emotional and intellectual upheaval, the national conscience
is being examined in a manner scarcely recognised in Britain. There
the ingrained jingoism of colonial centuries still keeps the hearts of
oak imperiously ticking over. In Ireland, garrulous argument still
hurtles forth in search of an accommodating national identity.

But the belief that Ireland now stands at a crossroads in its

45

history has been inspired not just by the election of Mary Robinson as President, or the debate on contraception that followed. It arises from the perception that Ireland is searching for a new equilibrium, trying to reconcile traditional nationalist and conservative politics with the demands and expectations of those growing up in a Europe which is more than an economic and agricultural cartel. Modern Europe is evolving common social attitudes and practice, and a body of law which increasingly touches everybody's life.

Of course, the mould of de Valeran conservatism was broken in the late Fifties when, after a period of stagnation and backwardness compared to the burgeoning economies of Europe in general and the United Kingdom in particular, the civil service led the political system in a dash for growth. Taoiseach Sean Lemass is remembered as the epitome of this generation, an unsentimental ex-revolutionary who re-established full trade links with Britain and sought friendship with the North. In this respect he was also among those who wished to revise the Republic's Constitution, making its claim to the Six Counties aspirational, and causing him to be regarded as the most radical of Fianna Fail politicians. But the apparent success of the new economic expansionism in its early days – it quickly generated growth in inward investment and employment – led to a rise in social expenditure that could not be sustained.

This partly explained the markedly pragmatic nature of Irish politics. Gone if not forgotten are the days of nationalist principle, of self-sufficiency, of economic patriotism, although they linger on in the Irish consumer's still marked preference for his native produce. In contrast to his British counterpart who is more promiscuous and eclectic, the Dubliner regards it as something of a betrayal to drink anything other than Irish whiskey or Irish mineral water or eat butter that is not Kerrygold. And it is hard to think of anyone with discerning taste buying other than Irish sausages.

Just as Ireland has successfully exploited Europe's Common Agricultural Policy, so it has been among the more skilful exponents of maintaining protectionism within the EC, whether through this residual consumer nationalism, or by imposing spurious environmental requirements on imported products, or by successfully defying the judgments of the European Court, as in its persistence in putting obstructions in the way of cross-border shopping at Newry. Nevertheless, despite such reluctance to embrace in full the principles of free trade (not without justification in a small and open economy), Ireland has been increasingly forced to accept its essentially semi-peripheral status in the European and international markets. Thus its financial autonomy is heavily restricted and dependent on decisions taken externally. Since the country relies so much on inward investment and international capital, which by 1986, according to the OECD, accounted for 40 per cent of Irish employment, it has had to offer very favourable terms. Repatriated profits do not in fact yield much revenue to the State which has spent heavily to attract the investment in the first place. According to critics of the Government in 1991, Irish corporation tax at ten per cent was considerably below the OECD average; in the other industrialised countries it was expected to yield about 2.7 per cent of GDP.

On one hand Dublin has seen fast industrialisation and developing consumerism along with a process of secularisation, which has moved more slowly than in comparable urban centres in Britain and Europe. But between these forces and the residual conservatism of its political and social system there is an obvious gulf. The often inert or impotent nature of Ireland's political parties and institutions reflects the fact that those groups which agitate for change are marginalised. The two major parties compete for votes right across the spectrum. In the UK coalitions are formed within the two great political parties (they each have their right and left wings) but their general tendency and thrust are clear. In Ireland the distinction is far less evident. All political systems require brokerage between competing interest groups, but in few countries can such inhibited brokerage (known in the vernacular as 'cute whooring') be more necessary and obvious, or lead more often to unpalatable or even ludicrous results. The failure of the divorce referendum, or Mr Haughey's abandonment of his old chum Brian Lenihan on the very eve of the Presidential election, are two obvious examples. A scornful Fine Gael opponent said of Fianna Fail during the budget debate in 1991: 'I often think that Fianna Fail is like a dependent society. In every town and village they encourage dependency and those who are most dependent vote Fianna Fail. They march them down to the polling booths and they vote for them in a despicable fashion. There is this problem with the whole ethos of the main Government party. We on this side of the House are the party of the hand up, not the party of the handout.'

Yet if Mr Haughey did not exist it would be necessary to invent him. His foxy wiles and pragmatism have aroused both admiration and contempt, and his apparent aspirations to statesmanship are often mocked. In March 1991 at his party's annual conference in Dublin, Mr Haughey tore many delegates out of their Rip van Winkle sleep with a speech which expressed his unexpected new vision of Ireland where tolerance, compassion and economic dynamism marched together to form a modern, pluralist State. It was strong stuff yet because of Mr Haughey's reputation for rampant opportunism, many observers automatically treated its substance with scepticism. John Waters in the *Irish Times* was one of the few commentators to argue otherwise: 'It is easy to be cynical about Mr Haughey's motivation: at this stage you might say he has little to lose, and perhaps a whole new political lifetime to gain, from coming on as the Great Progressive of Irish politics. But politicians can often be at their most useful when they have nothing to lose. Moreover, the vision and ideas articulated in Mr Haughey's speech are, in terms of the kind of politics which he himself has bequeathed us, quite staggering in their radicalism. If implemented, they would mean a far different and better Ireland – by almost any standards.'

Waters conceded that the ideas articulated by the Taoiseach were not new and that probably they had been espoused with far more passion than Mr Haughey, after a lifetime of political somersaults, could now muster. But he added: 'We have never heard them from the mouth of someone with such means at his disposal to turn them into reality.' What the Taoiseach was proposing, reflected Waters, was no less than total perestroika of Fianna Fail; in effect a new era of politics in Ireland. 'It is not too late for Mr Haughey to keep his nerve,' he argued, 'to leave his party colleagues reciting their rosaries and go about their business running the country in the manner desired by the majority of the people. In this, he deserves our support.'

Charles Haughey's claim to statesmanship has been enunciated on numerous occasions. Publication of *The Spirit of the Nation* somewhat pretentiously drew together his speeches between 1957 and 1986. Any British politician who offered publishers a selection of similar contributions from *Hansard* would get a dusty answer. In 1990 Mr Haughey suddenly emerged from a self-imposed period of purdah, as far as relations with the press were concerned, to give substantive interviews to the Irish newspapers. His most remarkable switch, and indeed one of his most remarkable achievements, is to have changed his approach to the economy so markedly. This once passionate advocate of social expenditure and denouncer of emigration, the classic way of moderating social and economic pressures in the country, came in turn to preside over a continuing haemorrhage of young and talented Irish people. When times have demanded it, he has also become an almost Thatcherite constrainer of the public purse. In *Understanding Modern Ireland*, a book published as recently as 1990, it was possible for four social scientists to conclude that Ireland was in crisis because its public programmes could not be sustained. Even by the time the book appeared the OECD was acknowledging the great success with which Ireland under Mr Haughey's leadership had turned the economy around, to the point where its rate of inflation was among the lowest in Europe and its rate of growth superior to that of the UK. Yet even by the end of 1990 the ratio of debt to Gross National Product remained at 111 per cent, though it had come down from 131 per cent as late as 1987. Social services had become less of a cuckoo in the nest than in the years when they accounted for half of public spending but they still claimed 45 per cent of all current expenditure in 1991. Just servicing the public debt was still absorbing 75 per cent of the revenue from income tax. The future was clouding again, with the uncertainties of the Gulf and an international recession. Indeed, the OECD had come to question whether Ireland could go on sustaining inward investment at such high cost. According to Fine Gael, over the last decade the State agencies had spent at least £5 billion in the promotion of industrial jobs but the number of jobs in the economy had actually declined by about 20,000 in that period. Inevitably the exceptionally low rate of corporate taxation increased the cost of the industrial policy and the burden on other taxpayers. The OECD put the question politely at the end of the decade: 'It might be asked whether Ireland has not now reached a stage of development at which heavy Government involvement in decisions on where to invest and which activities to support risks becoming counter-productive.'

In any period of economic change, of course, there are winners and losers, and as in other capitalist economies, the group that has suffered most are the socially dispossessed, that group with few aspirations locked into dismal public housing and welfare. This is

49

where the long-term unemployed are most likely to be found, and their housing subsidies have borne the brunt of cuts in State transfers, while reductions in other programmes, like health and education, most grievously damage this group because the poor have no power to exercise choice in the free market, an escape route available to those with better resources.

Understanding Contemporary Ireland, by Richard Breen, Damian F. Hannan, David B. Rottman, and Christopher T. Whelan (Gill and Macmillan, 1990) is the most recent and one of the most thoughtful academic attempts to understand this process. In the light of later experience the conclusions are perhaps excessively gloomy but they still carry much weight. These are that Ireland is in crisis. The State has come to play an over-centralised role in distributing economic opportunities and yet has been 'monumentally unsuccessful' either in ensuring sustained economic growth or in moderating social inequalities.

In a recent keynote lecture on Church and State at Queen's University, Belfast, Dr Noel Browne, one of Ireland's foremost intellectuals and the controversial Minister of Health in the first coalition Government of 1948–1951, delivered an eloquent but blistering attack on the Irish status quo: 'At the conclusion of the fiasco of our own 75 years of freedom in the South we have created a manifestly unjust, ineptly run society, in which 20 per cent of the people are constantly unemployed. Two in three of our people – men, women and children – live at or below the poverty line. With no work, thousands of our unwanted young people must emigrate. Because of cuts in the health service, there are 41,000 hospital beds lying empty needed by patients waiting for attention. O'Connell Street in Dublin has been described as the "largest psychiatric out-patient clinic in the country". Old bagmen and old bagwomen are tumbled into the streets where, with young unwanted children, in their hundreds, they beg to survive for the day, and sleep rough at night in all weathers. The Irish are said to be the highest percentage of those – Scots, Welsh and English – in London's Cardboard City.'

The authors of *Understanding Modern Ireland* trace the beginning of this crisis to the economic and political inertia that sapped Irish initiatives at the end of the war when the rest of Europe was embarking on a period of rapid social and economic change. Under de Valeran leadership Ireland had consolidated its national autonomy and independence but at some cost. The Catholic Church had been given a dominant role both in determining social policy and delivering education. Protectionism had favoured a bourgeoisie classically deriving its wealth from its own small businesses but had led it into inefficiency, stagnation and decline. The civil service had adopted from its British inheritance the tradition of Treasury control and its strict containment of State expenditures, as well as the State's acceptance of an auxiliary, rather than a decisive, role in economic activity or the supply of services.

By the middle of the Fifties the economic crisis could not be hidden. Indeed Breen *et al.* conclude that all the State's economic policies were bankrupt. Between 1949 and 1956 the gross national products of the European democracies had grown at eight per cent. Ireland faced crises in the balance of payments and high inflation. Industry and agriculture both declined. About 400,000 people emigrated, mainly to Britain, during the decade. About one person in every five born since independence and resident in 1951 had emigrated by the end of the decade, and for those in the younger age groups the rate of departure was nearly twice as great. Indeed, in many years emigrants almost equalled the number of births.

But Ireland made a decisive break in 1958 when it adopted economic planning, with the publication of the *Programme for Economic Expansion*. Suddenly the State as diffident and parsimonious godfather was dead; it was now fixer and provider, luring movers and shakers in an increasingly internationalised economy to pitch their tents in Ireland. The results were dramatic. In the first ten years of economic planning GNP grew by 50 per cent and the size of the civil service by 25 per cent. Public spending also soared, from 30 to 40 per cent of GDP. With some pause enforced by the oil shock of 1974, the growth continued steadily until by 1980 the total public domain accounted for nearly a third of the workforce. Borrowing, much of it from abroad, maintained the momentum and by 1982 public expenditure had reached 64 per cent of GDP with about half of it devoted to social services.

By now it was also becoming clear that this extraordinary period of economic boom was having a profound effect on the class system. Late and rapid industrialisation meant that Ireland was unable to compensate for the decline of agriculture, with emigration filling the gap. In two decades from 1961 the proportion of male farm labour halved while white-collar positions doubled to almost 15 per cent, though at 16 per cent the contribution of farming to employment remains much higher than in Britain. The State through its fiscal and industrial policies discriminated in favour of the proprietorial class or the external investor, helping to create a new bourgeoisie of managerial and service professionals owing their economic fealty often to foreign corporations.

In contrast a number of groups suffered. People on moderate incomes were brought more and more into the tax system because allowances were not indexed, leading to increasing bitterness and resentment among PAYE earners. Some estimates claim that between 11 per cent and 18 per cent of those living in poverty are nevertheless paying tax on income which in more than half the cases quoted in 1991 amounted to £20 a week or more.

Large farmers not only benefited from the tax system but prospered from State investments in agricultural production and marketing, and entry into the EC much reduced their dependence on British markets, but the large traditional troop of relatives who helped on family farms had been leaving the land in big numbers; and in general small and marginal farmers became the beneficiaries of EC and Government policies aimed not at creating profits, but supplementing incomes to prevent the destruction of their lifestyle. The smallholder with his turf, his few cattle, and his donkey still clings to the soil but only with the help of the State.

However, the chief victims of the explosive changes in the Irish economy were people without skills or educational attainments, the group that analysts of capitalist systems everywhere identify as the underclass. And the Dublin working class was victim of change twice over, for the new industrial incentives were designed to locate industries in growth points outside the capital. Breen *et al.* note: 'This policy was greatly to the detriment of the Dublin working class. The industrial employment opportunities available to them and their children were concentrated in the old indigenous Irish industry, which fared poorly in the post-1958 era relative to the new industries attracted through the State's development policies. So the traditional urban working class was effectively marginalised in the course of economic development, without opportunities for manual work and unable to compete for the white collar positions being created on their doorsteps.'

Furthermore, the authors argue, the thrust of State spending and transfers discriminated in favour of those at the top of the class system. In other words, the State's intervention was redistributive but not in the direction usually sought by such policies in other countries. Although the increase in social spending allowed the State to underwrite, to some degree, the lives of poor farmers and unskilled labourers, the irony was that the most substantial support went to already privileged people in the bureaucracy or the liberal professions. Those who provided health care, education and community welfare experienced a big rise in their incomes. The net effect is that policies widened class disparities and then ensured their continuation.

To some extent the reductions in public spending that have taken place since the authors reached their gloomy findings have affected the bourgeois groups as well. Health and education cuts leave their marks on teachers and doctors. The crisis in Larry Goodman's cattle empire in 1990, precipitated by the Gulf War and Iraq's failure to meet its debts, revealed the extent to which the State supported the proprietorial class and indeed, some suggest, connived at its exploitation – to the point of impropriety – of EC and State funds. But it is perhaps unlikely that the banks, or indeed the Government, can ever again afford to take so complacent a view of economic indiscipline and laxity.

In his book *Ireland, a Social and Cultural History* (Fontana), Terence Brown notes that Ireland went through a very rapid transformation in the Sixties and the Seventies, making a switch from being a primarily rural, agricultural society to an industrial, urban society. By 1971 more than half the population lived in towns and the growth of Dublin was the most marked. By now a third of the country's population lived in the capital. But there was an ambivalence in the change. Most of the newcomers were ready and able to take part in Dublin's growing bureaucratic and service economy, as white collar workers or professionals, yet at the same time the old labouring and unskilled classes were being edged into the urban wilderness. Terence Brown discusses this 'oddly ambiguous' aspect of the new Irish society in the following terms: 'Undoubtedly in the Sixties and Seventies many experienced living standards higher than any they had known in the past, but poor housing conditions, in bleak, ill-planned areas of the major cities were settings for vandalism, drug abuse, petty crime and lives of quiet desperation in the way of city life in much of the developed world. Despite the economic improvements of the last two decades, poverty, particularly in the inflation-dogged Seventies, has scarred the lives of many Irishmen and women in years when social progress, the outcome of increased opportunities in a modernising society, was assumed to be a primary contemporary fact.'

Long-term unemployment and the poverty trap continue to preoccupy the political parties, and beneath Dublin's international sophistication and consumerist delight there is evidence to bear out some commentators' gloomier conclusions. South Dublin, with its affluent suburbs of Ballsbridge, Foxrock, Dalkey and Killiney, has clearly been the beneficiary of the rising wealth of the diplomatic class and the new bourgeoisie of favoured proprietors, professionals and entrepreneurs sardonically banded together as the 'thinking scampi set'. But hidden pockets in the south and the disintegrating fabric of the north of the city tell, in many streets, a different story. Here elegant terraces lean into the twilight of visible decay. Planning blight creeps over them like a disease insidiously killing some noble tree. But since its Millenium in 1988 Dublin has made efforts to restore its structure. Public buildings have been deftly patched and cleaned, yet the laxity of the planning laws – and the failure for so long to introduce smoke-control – have given it much ground to recover.

However, the bourgeoisie so favoured by the State has not been kind to Dublin. Some social chroniclers suggest that the neglect of Dublin and its Georgian inheritance reflects an underlying dislike for its symbolism of the ascendancy. The architectural critic of the *Financial Times*, in a famous passage quoted by Colm Toibin in *Dubliners* (Macdonald Illustrated, 1990), wrote: 'The only reason why Dublin remained for so long the beautiful eighteenth-century city the English built is that the Irish were too poor to knock it down. This, unfortunately, is no longer the case.'

Dublin, noted Toibin, was not part of a 'great national heritage', or a haven for Irish speakers. It was, in many ways, a British city. Once the new money came in it was easy prey and over the the next 30 years the city centre, with the exception of Fitzwilliam and Merrion Squares on the South Side, were made unrecognisable by the developers. Protests tended to be dismissed as arising from that unholy alliance of the genteel and the left-wing. Meanwhile, as the city centre was being abandoned to the smash-and-grab instincts of the property speculators and the office developers, a new Dublin was arising, the novelist Dermot Bolger's hidden Dublin to which the poor were consigned, often without proper facilities or infra-structure. Professor R.F. Foster, in his *Modern Ireland 1600–1972* (Allen Lane, 1988), commented: 'Weak and belated planning laws had not halted the ruination of many rural and urban amenities; organisations like An Foras Forbeartha (National Institution for Physical Planning and Construction Research) and An Taisce (the National Trust for Ireland) could do little against combined avarice and apathy, though the ultimate lunacy of a Dublin "traffic scheme" that suggested concreting in the Grand Canal was dropped. Inner-city Dublin tenements were displaced to high-rise slums in distant suburbs.' Hence the glowering, punitive and unruly towers of North Dublin's Ballymun.

In all of this Dublin was by no means unique in Europe. It was a common enough error after the war in London, Glasgow, Edinburgh and other major cities in Britain. But whereas in the UK the response was the development of legislation to conserve the best of what was left, Ireland's reaction was more passive and belated. Rather than a backlash against the Ascendancy, its conservation lethargy more probably reflected another characteristic of the State: its reluctance until more recent times to interfere in the normal commercial processes. For a long time before its inter-ventionist phase, the Government regarded itself as the distant regulator and patron of agencies and individuals. Just as it deferred to the Church on questions of social policy so it deferred to business on entrepreneurial questions. Indeed, as previously discussed, the whole thrust of its economic policies discriminated in favour of the commercial class. The fact that Mr Haughey made a fortune in property speculation in Dublin did not cause the weakness of planning legislation but it did not prevent it, either. In this Mr Haughey was not alone. But to suggest that the neglect of Georgian Dublin was a deliberate act underestimates the outrage so many Dubliners did feel about it. At least, the worst of the philistine impulse seems to have passed, and conservation and the spirit of civic improvement are now more obviously alive as Dublin vigorously pursues its destiny as an international capital. And despite its obvious sores, this new and pleasing bricks-and-mortar promise is enabling more Dubliners themselves to renew a sense of pride and participation in a city large enough to be cosmopolitan but still sufficiently small to avoid the wretched anonymity of being remote.

6

SCENES
Statues

DUBLIN IS a great place for turning heroes to stone and any traipse around its monumental offspring should commence with the bluster of O'Connell Street where the wind whips up off the Liffey to send pedestrians gusting along Bachelors' Walk and Eden Quay. With his left hand tucked inside his frock coat, in the manner of Napoleon, Daniel O'Connell, the 19th-century champion of Catholic Emancipation, and early agitator for Irish independence, surveys a city vastly altered since that of his 'monster meetings' in 1843. Then he addressed the eager multitudes in his campaign for repeal of the Union which tethered Ireland to Britain.

Up on top of the pedestal O'Connell's Herculean frame displays a romantic sense of authority. He was one of the few Catholic barristers in the land and the cloak of learning is draped around his shoulders; law books and the tomes of politics and philosophy are at his feet. The sculptors Foley and Brock have given him a benign head with faintly dimpled cheeks and the eyes cast, it must be said, in the direction of Virgin Records on Aston Quay. On the granite base of the monument rests a huge cylindrical pedestal around which are clustered saints and scholars and various mythological folk including Erin trampling her cast-off fetters under foot and holding the Act of Emancipation in her left hand. At the four corners of the base winged maidens – Fidelity, Patriotism, Eloquence and Justice – sit in courtly attention.

'O'Connell had a stately presence,' wrote Justin Huntley McCarthy in his *Short History of Our Times*. 'A face capable of expressing easily and effectively the most rapid alterations of mood, and a voice which all hearers admit to having been almost unrivalled for strength and sweetness.'

In this central aisle of the street with its ornate lamp-posts, William Smith O'Brien stands behind the vast bulk of O'Connell in slenderly athletic contrast. With his arms folded lightly across his chest, and his fine aquiline profile, he seems almost effete but here indeed was one of the most prominent members of the Young Irelanders, condemned to death for high treason in 1848 for his role in an unsuccessful insurrection against British rule. The sentence was lifted, however, and O'Brien lived until 1864. Following behind there is Sir John Gray, proprietor of the *Freeman's Journal*, whose commemorative statue at the junction of O'Connell and Abbey Streets appears somewhat avuncular. In one hand he holds the stem of what seems to be a pipe. Gray, with O'Connell and many others, was sent to Richmond Prison in England during the Repeal Agitation, but the Lords revoked the sentence and they were set at liberty. From 1860 to 1875 he was chairman of the Dublin Corporation Waterworks, and was largely instrumental in procuring the city's water supply: a vital contribution in a place resplendent with Georgian grandeur, but struggling to improve the lot of those cornered by festering poverty.

A few footfalls to the left of the street there is the General Post Office with its ionic portico supporting a pediment set with the figures of Hibernia, Mercury and Fidelity. Although the interior of the building was completely destroyed during the Easter Rising of 1916, the façade is almost entirely original. Inside the memorial to those who died defending the building during the rebellion takes the form of Cuchullain, the redoubtable warrior of Irish legend. Outside and back again on the centre walkway of the street, the granite gravitas of the earlier statues is ruptured suddenly by the grand crumpled exuberance of James Larkin's monument. Here, on top of his plinth, encased in the creased resilience of his working man's serge suit, Larkin stands with his arms outstretched in the passionate style of an Italian tenor. He could be singing an aria but he is offering the trade unionist's benediction, his mouth set in a roar of exhortation: 'The great appear great because we are on our knees . . . let us rise.'

This is the face of hardship, a squashed, battered face still seen amid the rundown housing of the Liberties and also the deprived areas of cities like Liverpool and Glasgow which lent support during Larkin's bitter and bloody Transport and General Workers' strike of 1913. On either side of his stocky pillar there are salutations from two literary compadres. On the left these words from Sean O'Casey: 'He talked to the workers, spoke as only Jim Larkin could speak, not for an assignation with peace, dark obedience or placid resignation; but trumpet-tongued of resistance to wrong, discontent with leering poverty, and defiance of any power strutting out to stand in the way of their march onward.' On the right side of the plinth the poet Patrick Kavanagh offers his own particular appreciation:

> And tyranny trampled them in Dublin's gutter
> Until Jim Larkin came along and cried
> The call of Freedom and the call of pride
> And slavery crept to its hands and knees
> And Nineteen Thirteen cheered from out the utter
> Degradation of their miseries.

Moving on from Larkin, one sometimes treads the ground of shifting pavement artists before reaching one of the crudest aberrations in Dublin's monumental art. But first the chalked-up insight of a sidewalk philosopher who offers A Story About the Punt: 'In days gone by young men (made of iron) used to take their beloved out on the river in punts, talking sweet gibberish and frequently falling backwards into the river whilst punting. Today young men (made of man-made fibre) take their beloved to a pub throwing her punts over the bar, frequently falling backwards. How times have changed.' (The punt is, of course, the Irish pound.)

No escape now from the nauseous vision of Anna Livia, Anna Liffey, the female manifestation of Dublin's powerful old river. Nelson's Pillar, a fluted column in the Doric style surmounted by a colossal statue of the admiral, once rose loftily over O'Connell Street close to this spot. Spiral stairs led to a railed platform at the top, providing a wonderful panoramic view of the city bounded by the bay to the east, by the Carlingford and Mourne mountains to the north and by the Dublin hills and Wicklow mountains to the south-west and south. From 1806 to 1966 (when Nelson was detonated by IRA sympathisers in the dead of night without injury to anyone), the pillar stood as a colonial imperative to a nation which had little reverence for the man aloft. But its style did at least command artistic respect, so much so that after its explosion several sharp-witted buckos in the city claimed to have come by the head of 'old one-eye' in a garden shed and, the lads let it be known, any curio collector offering a decent price would be seriously considered. By the end of the year there must have been at least a dozen heads of Nelson going the round of the *aficionados*, each one claimed as the genuine article.

For decades no statue occupied the space left by the pillar's demolition. Then the mightily rich Smurfits, one of Dublin's leading immigrant industrialist dynasties, decided to stake out the location for a civic work given by the family to commemorate the city's Millenium in 1988. So Anna Livia emerged but not in the heroic or seductive shape that most of Dublin would wish upon her. Instead she appears in galling mediocrity, instantly mocked as 'The Floozie in the Jacuzzi' or, by the harsher-tongued: 'The whoor in the sewer'. She is an ill-proportioned creature, afflicted by a gangrenous-green patina which is rippled continuously by water pouring from a series of spouts. The work is contained in a sort of sarcophagus of staggered granite blocks, giving the whole construction something of the ambience of a Stalinesque public lavatory.

As if holding up his hands in mute alarm at the cold, crude nakedness of this lamentable Anna Liffey, the pale, weather-beaten figure of Father Matthew, the Apostle of Temperance, stands behind. In the second quarter of the 19th century Matt Talbot wielded great influence in Ireland in the unlikely matter of sobriety. This statue of white marble was modelled by Mary Redmond and unveiled in 1893. On each hand fingers are missing from the middle joints, bitten off by almost a century of wind and driving rain. But Father Matt still has his eyes about him, keeping vigilant watch on a wedding party pouring out of the Gresham Hotel, wreathed in Calvin Klein's 'Obsession' and cigar smoke and the sharp, bright shine of designer apparel.

At the corner of North Earl Street and O'Connell Street, James Joyce, his hat characteristically tilted, defies the block of metal holding down his feet to rise in sprightly greeting of the day. Even so the props of advancing years are not forgotten in Marjorie

Fitzgibbon's statue. Joyce rests on a stick, and a pair of spectacles are balanced before his merciless, myopic eyes squinting in the direction of the GPO.

Then onwards to another shrine, but one of less sceptical inclination. Under a glass frame the red and white statue of the Sacred Heart is placed between two small sprays of fabric flowers. There is an exultant kitschness here that could make this a roadside altar in any Mediterranean country, and although modern Catholicism sets no store by the theory of indulgences today, a notice inside the frame informs the faithful that the invocation, 'Sacred Heart of Jesus, I place my trust in Thee', carries, according to Pope Pius X, a 300-day reprieve from Purgatory: a sort of sanctified time off for good behaviour. Pinned next to this humble holy corner is a notice to taxi-drivers advertising the more temporal nourishment of Sounds Restaurant on Bolton Street, open 20 hours a day for mugs of strong tea and traditional fries. 'Give us a try, we won't disappoint.' But the shrine itself is a reminder that Dublin, for all its impudent anti-clericalism, is still the capital of a deeply spiritual country. An ambulance tears along O'Connell Street, sirens wailing, and a message boy on the pavement crosses himself in prayer.

Just in front of the Gate Theatre and close by the Rotunda – the first maternity hospital in the entire British Isles, as it then was – a triangular shaft of Galway granite rises 60 feet in the air, surmounted by a flaming torch. This is the Parnell monument, and on a pedestal there is the man himself, the gentleman patriot whose endowment of political charisma and aloof handsomeness made him the dominant personality in Irish history during the 1880s and 1890s. With its outstretched right arm raised as if in an oratorical blessing, Gaudens' bronze statue evokes something of Parnell's reputation for superbly gauged gestures and theatrical reticence. But behind him, on the granite needle, are the words which soared forth from those moments of dramatic silence:

No man has the right to fix the boundary to the march of the nation.
No man has the right to say to his country
Thus far shalt thou go and no further.
We have never attempted to fix the ne-plus-ultra
To the progress of Ireland's nationhood, and we never shall.

At his feet, the inheritors of this vision are lurching towards progress in buses and cars, engrossed in the kind of struggle Charles Stewart Parnell could never have imagined – the curse of traffic jams.

7

THEMES
Women and Countess Markievicz

WOMEN IN IRELAND have always been powerful in that pervasive but unshowy way of the kitchen politician, turning smiling, subservient faces to their menfolk in the outer world but within the intimate shadows of the home dispensing the subtle wisdom of a lifetime's watching and listening. Yet such covert authority often provides no long-term benefits to anyone. For when the shibboleths of male self-interest prevent women from openly entering into the thick of things then society's aspirations and definitions of itself become unbalanced and women's only lever on power may be reduced to the craft of whispering within the family.

But Mary Robinson's extraordinary triumph in becoming Ireland's first woman President has challenged retrograde separatism. Although the Presidency is entirely symbolic, having a woman in the job has already proved tremendously beneficial psychologically to other women. It provides, at last, a national endorsement of women's own increasing confidence and their determination to transcend the confines of private life to be fully represented in a public world. So the quest to nurture equilibrium between the sexes is on.

'As a woman, I want women who have felt themselves outside history to be written back into history,' President Robinson said during her inaugural address. 'In the words of [*the poet*] Eavan Boland, "finding a voice where they have found a vision".' In no other western democracy could the desire of women to be written back into history be expressed with such authenticity. This is not the cry of hyperbolic feminism but the imperative of a section of the electorate which until the legal campaigns of Mary Robinson and the lobbying of the women's movement in Dublin from 1971 had no access to contraception, no right to sit on juries, and in the case of single or separated parents no entitlements to welfare payments. Until as recently as 1986 illegitimacy still carried official stigma in Ireland and, although membership of the European Community brought more change in social attitudes than had occurred in the previous half century, the Republic remains the only nation within the Community where divorce is banned by the Constitution and abortion on any grounds is still a criminal act.

Over generations, since the founding of the State in 1922, inequality was so automatically wedged into the system (allegedly for the economic and moral good of a small, emergent country), that right up to the Seventies women in many careers, including banking and the civil service, had to resign from their jobs on marriage. In fact women's role as wives was defined almost exclusively as that of child-rearers. In a society still motivated by the clenched idealism of Eamon de Valera in alliance with a right-wing hierarchy, women were reduced to second-class citizenship, the victims of punitive, man-made Mariolatry (adoration of the Madonna), which both inflicted guilt and stoked it with a furious interpretation of virtue, leaving women with practically only one conduit for individual pleading – the secret, urgent intentions of private prayer.

But by March 1971 in Dublin the momentum for change among women breached the barricades that Ireland had constructed from taboos. The first structural cracks appeared during Gay Byrne's compulsive television programme, *The Late Late Show*, when a discussion on the status of women between guests and the audience unleashed such rage at the injustices, such waves of hitherto suppressed pain, that the studio switchboard was overrun with calls not just from the city but from all over the country. As a result of the publicity the women's movement called a meeting in the Lord Mayor's Mansion House in Dublin and more than a thousand people gathered there to register support. June Levine, the journalist and founder member of the group, notes in her study, *Sisters*, that: 'We'd turned women on. We'd revealed the underground anger in women's lives, we'd blown the cover.'

'O commemorate me with no hero-courageous
Tomb – just a canal-bank seat for the passer-by . . .'

A lunchtime lounger on the banks of the Grand Canal, where seats are
dedicated to the poet, Patrick Kavanagh, and the composer, Percy French

The Tallaght Youth Band marching towards the General Post Office in
O'Connell Street on Saturday afternoon

The fashion designer John Rocha and his wife and business partner, Odette, at home in Rafarnham, outside Dublin, with Zoe, Simone and Max

A didgeridoo jig on Grafton Street

The amiable porters' desk at the Shelbourne Hotel

Banjo-ist with a bracing melody on Dun Laoghaire's East Pier

Charlie and Mariad Whisker, painter and fashion designer, amid the leafy loveliness of a rolling garden surrounded by meadows, hedgerows and hills

Dublin still has its corners of grand style as depicted in Fox's tobacco shop on Graftron Street

The light and shade of Dublin striking the Parnell Monument in O'Connell Street

A bundle of bicycles in the courtyard of Trinity College

The Forty Foot at Sandycove, a bathing point for briney stoics

Eccles Street, the territory of James Joyce's fictional boulevardier, Leopold Bloom, who lived at No 7, now supplanted by the private wing of the Mater Hospital

Sacred Kitsch on O'Connell Street

Urchins in Sean MacDermott Street

Blown the cover . . . but not destroyed the patriarchal bigotry. That very same month Dr John Charles McQuaid, Archbishop of Dublin, was writing the following in a pastoral letter read to congregations: 'Any such contraceptive act is always wrong in itself. To speak then . . . of a right to contraception on the part of an individual, be he Christian or non-Christian or atheist, or on the part of a minority or a majority, is to speak of a right that cannot exist. [*Legalising contraceptives*] . . . would be an insult to our Faith . . . a curse upon our country.' With cries of 'Rubbish', some men as well as women, marched out from the pews, and while reactionary politicians and clerics continued their crude condemnation of change, women in Dublin increasingly found the courage to oppose the whole crushing burden of traditional authority, its contempt for personal independence and its old trick of intimidation by guilt.

Today, although justice for all in Ireland remains in the making, much has improved. 'Ten years ago I doubt if there was more than one woman barrister in Dublin,' reflects Rita Childers, widow of the former much-esteemed President Erskine Childers. 'Now the place seems to be teeming with them and their excellence is widely noted.' But in some quarters sneers are still lobbed against women's march towards equality and their desire to dislodge the discredited values of a complacent, unthinking status quo. However, the very offensiveness of these insults suggests an antiquated order under threat. As an example of raw panic there is little to surpass some of the anti-woman abuse hurled at Mary Robinson by Fianna Fail during the Presidential campaign in the winter of 1990. Despite her insistence that she personally is not in favour of abortion but does believe in every woman's right to information, John Browne, the Fianna Fail politician, announced that her Presidency would turn the official residence, Aras an Uachtarain, into an abortion referral clinic.

There followed further insubstantial stories that Mary Robinson and her husband Nick, a lawyer, were separating. Then came the most pernicious attack of all. In the course of a radio programme the Environment Minister, Padraig Flynn, announced that: 'None of those who knew Mary Robinson in a previous incarnation ever heard her claiming to be a great wife.' Surfacing here was that primitive smear which implies that a woman with a career must be a negligent spouse. But, in the words 'previous incarnation', there was also the hidden criticism of Mary Robinson's appearance at the

Presidential hustings. Previously not known for her dress sense, she now had poise and elegance which suggested public relations grooming and therefore a manufactured candidate.

Yet what such personal accusations and innuendo always betray is a certain kind of man's innate fear of brainy women. However, in the attempts to damage President Robinson's character, the jibes were a palpable failure. In Dublin especially public anger was immediate and protests were ignited right across party lines. In fact the fury was soon evident throughout the country and the self-damage of Flynn's blunder was seen by his almost instant retraction. Thus the only heartening aspect of the episode was its indication of a shift in social opinions; the public wanted none of this squalid rhetoric and said so. Fianna Fail's dirty-tricks brigade had badly misjudged the prevailing mood.

Despite the braggart infamy of Dublin particularly, but also the country as a whole, Ireland, sitting out in the Atlantic, battered by rain and the gales of history, has always been irrefutably female: the earth mother ornamented with heroic pet names like Cathleen ni Houlihan and Roisin Dubh, breeding rebel sons and powerful prelates, and politicians who adore their mammies but perceive approaching feminists as more perilous than sin. As in Italy this excessive mother-cult has bred a man's country where even today young Dublin women will tell you, 'Sons are kings', and only a few years ago Michael D. Higgins, the Labour politician and women's rights activist, was still able to write: 'I could take you to rural communities where single women with no dowries remain stuck at home and are remembered in the will with a room in the house and a seat in the cart to Mass.'

But this feeling of the city as a male preserve defines even Dublin's literary establishment where women writers of significant talent still sometimes find difficulty in gaining recognition within the literary mainstream. As a consequence very few women ever seem to be listed in the Irish book awards, not, one suspects, because their creativity and style don't merit inclusion but because the often personal nature of their writing finds little appreciation among the panels of sponsors and critics, the majority of whom are men. Over the years the British novelist Fay Weldon has been involved in judging some of the awards and in her view: 'Irishmen aren't interested in the kind of subjects many Irish women write about, so they refuse to call it literature.' In the Sixties the novelist

Edna O'Brien, writing explicitly about the impulses of female sexuality, love and betrayal, found she was also taking on the Dublin literati. 'God, they got the razors out,' she once remarked. Nevertheless there can be little dispute today that one of the most exciting voices in new Irish writing belongs to Anne Enright, born in Dublin 30 years ago, and the author of *The Portable Virgin*, whose witty, forthright and subversive stories possess a spare, un-emotional force rarely evident in contemporary writing in Ireland.

Sinéad O'Connor's cold candour on issues affecting Irish women is equally integral to this search for equilibrium between the sexes, this driven wish to be rid of stage-Irish blethering and codology, and that special mind-freeze on equality which hardens into an expectancy of failure. Her frankness in defending a woman's right to choose on the abortion issue, her loud contempt for the Government's inadequate health campaign against AIDS, her condemnation of the Catholic Church for 'centuries of imperialism and oppression' . . . such outbursts have broadened Sinéad O'Connor's impact beyond her chosen world of rock music. Like Mary Coughlan, whose songs of disturbing unsentimentality contain something of the potency of France's Edith Piaf, O'Connor has made a quantum leap from the prissily innocent colleen strumming her harp, once so beloved of the Irish Tourist Board's mythology.

But will the Ireland of such radical yet disparate spirits as O'Connor and President Robinson really be a better, more homogeneous place? Or will it simply emerge as another sullen and me-oriented society – like America or Britain where feminism after 20 years of marching towards the light now seems in retreat among the young? One man who believes all the social questioning is bound to be for the country's good is Dermot Bolger, the award-winning Dublin novelist and playwright, some of whose work often exposes a tyrannous male ignorance about women. 'I'm very sure that by electing a woman to lead us we have said: "This will be our decade of maturity and achievement." For economic reasons the young still have to emigrate but they travel well. Many of those young women who leave are extremely well educated and civilised, and ultimately they want to bring their skills back here to secure a tolerant, self-confident society.' The new Irish woman isn't pushy in the same way as her American counterpart, Bolger observes, but she will still carry tremendous influence.

In Dublin alone, though, a fair measure of positive discrimination is still required to counter career-management imbalance. In 1992 the second Commission on the Status of Women will produce a comprehensive study but already seven of its interim recommendations have been accepted 'in principle' by the Taoiseach. These range from required legislation for the joint ownership of the family home to the raising of the job application age to 50 in the public sector, and the immediate cessation of National Lottery, or other public, funds to golf clubs and other social amenities which discriminate against women. But even with future improvements women may still find, as they have done all over the world, that the enshrinement of equality in law is not always enough. The throwback mentality of a ruling mediocrity with its vested interests, office intrigue and sexual treachery will continue to work to keep them off the executive ladder. But if, as a result, women continue to set their sights low, then that in itself is almost a betrayal of Mary Robinson's victory. By her determined beavering forward, the President has irrefutably proved that women are worth all the things that men are worth. The choice for everyone, she had said, is between Ireland as a backwater republic of nudge-and-wink, or Ireland as a shining state in a new Europe. In the end the real enemy of women is inertia.

CLOSE ON 75 YEARS ago a member of the Protestant Irish aristocracy in Dublin transcended the throttling etiquette of her day to become the first of her sex to win a seat at Westminster, the Mother of Parliaments. In her advocacy of rebellion Constance Markievicz never participated in the House of Commons and so her record as a pioneer in this respect has been overshadowed by an equally imperious contemporary, Nancy Astor, immortalised in history as the first woman politician actually to take her British Parliamentary seat. Not that Countess Markievicz could have done the same, anyway. At the time of her General Election triumph in the Dublin constituency of St Patrick in 1918, she was residing in Holloway Prison. Ireland at that time was still under British domination, still binding up the wounds of the abortive Easter Rising which, two years before, had ransacked Dublin both mentally and physically.

Along with more than 100 fellow Sinn Feiners, including

de Valera, Markievicz had been arrested, and interned in Holloway without trial. The pretext, in her case, was her alleged involvement with a German plot, but none of this prevented the despatch of the official letter requesting her to take her constituency place at Westminster. This was delivered to her in a squalid cell, the incongruity of the episode heightened by the letter's signature, Lloyd George. But since Sinn Fein had decided to boycott the Commons and form its own republican parliament, Dail Eireann, there never was any probability that the Red Countess would become a Westminster regular. Yet firebrand that she was, she was also humanly nosey and egocentric enough to creep incognito into the House, during a later convalescent stay in London, to examine her name plate under its allocated coatpeg in the members' cloakroom.

In the pantheon of Irish heroes Constance Markievicz occupies only a marginal position, and abroad her name is scarcely recognised at all. Of the 90 women who responded to the patriot Padraig Pearse's call to join Dublin's Rising in 1916 only one carried a gun, the Countess who was born in England and took up arms at St Stephen's Green in Dublin where she was Chief Lieutenant throughout the fighting. But although the role of women was notable during the insurrection, male ambition had elbowed it into the sidelines by 1917. The historian Margaret McCurtain argues that the Irish Proclamation was considerably feminist in tone, recognising not only the right of every child but also the right to the franchise for women throughout the country. 'But by 1917 there is no doubt that there was a growing distancing of the political men from the women of the nation,' she says. Markievicz, the world's first woman Minister of Labour, belonged to the Cabinet in the first Dail but by the second Dail she had been removed. James Connolly, commander of the Irish Citizen Army during the Rising, had shown considerable solidarity with the women's movement of the time, but with his execution women's issues became obscured. 'I don't think women took the time to stand back and see what was happening,' reflects McCurtain. 'It was only when their male colleagues were in power that they realised what was going on. They tried to fight their corner, but because of the Civil War there was no longer unity among them to fight on a women's card.' Mysogyny, in fact, permeated the country during the 1920s, so much that in 1927 women were excluded from the Juries Act on the pretext that they were more accustomed to the private and domestic side of Irish life, and therefore not eligible to participate beyond those vistas.

The author Diana Norman argues a persuasive case, in her book *Terrible Beauty*, for recognising Markievicz as a pivotal international figure in the advancement of women and the Labour movement. The fact that she is generally remembered today only as an upper-class eccentric who fell in love with militant socialism is, in Norman's view, an extreme example of 'the process by which women are denigrated until they disappear from history'. Nevertheless the Countess's braying lack of tact and haughty aura must have irritated many of those whose pitiful condition she strove to share. But with its detailed research and perceptive analysis Norman's portrait reveals a strong, generous-hearted heroine who was quite genuinely affected by the miseries of a world which was the polar opposite of her own.

She belonged to the Gore-Booths of Lissadell, north of Sligo, and, anxious from an early age to escape the tally-ho enthusiasms of her set, she went to Paris to study art. There in the more reckless, but equally self-regarding, world of bohemia she became entranced by Casimir Markievicz. Initially the rapture was mutual and they married, but every trip back to Dublin increased Constance's naïve zeal for Irish politics while at the same time diminishing the passion she had felt for the urbane Polish count. Campaigns became her imperative rather than the careless café society to which Casimir belonged. Inevitably they parted, a separation that was relatively amicable, given the mores of the age. And so, at the age of 40, Constance ('a living Rossetti or Burne-Jones', in the words of one of Casi's friends) turned her noble shoulders against both the enticements of Paris and the social whirl and privilege of the Irish Ascendancy. Instead she took up arms and eventually endured five prison sentences mostly in dank jails where she produced a series of poignant water colours. The death penalty, imposed for her role in the Rising, was commuted to life but in that instance she only served 14 months. Yet the old extrovert flourish was never entirely extinguished.

During the Rebellion she had rashly signified her rank of lieutenant by attaching a lavish feather to her slouch cap. Such showiness, as Diana Norman observes, should indeed have made her an easy target but she came through unscathed which, perhaps, didn't say much for British military marksmanship. But as much as anything it was that lapse into vanity which earned her little besides derision in certain Dublin quarters. There were plenty who delighted in dismissing her as no more than a society woman parading about the city in fancy dress. But Dublin's begrudgery can be a fickle thing. When Markievicz, by then a Catholic, died in 1927 at the age of 59 the city turned out by the thousand to file past her coffin. Norman notes that it was as if all the quarrelling in the infant Republic had just for a few hours submerged its bitterness to march in this extraordinary woman's funeral procession. Today there is a plaque at 49 Leinster Road, Rathmines, in Dublin, recalling that the house was once her address. All around is flatland now, the bedsitter world of single civil servants, teachers and nurses, rather than the hideouts of impetuous patriots plotting anarchy into the dawn.

If she had taken her seat in the House of Commons would Countess Markievicz have found Lady Astor a comradely sister or a sartorial foe? Nancy always wore hats in the Chamber, not to be noticeably chic necessarily, but just to be noticeable. With Constance in her outrageous cap what melodrama those two women would have brought to that glumly apparelled throng.

FROM THE days of the warrior queen Maeve to the Dublin beauty Constance Markievicz and Yeats's firebrand muse Maude Gonne, Irish women have never been slow to prove their valour or inspire the best work in great novelists, playwrights and poets. Mother Ireland breathing warm and lively blessings on her children's dreams, a handsome, restive, war-bedraggled comrade of their thirsts for freedom, yet still a tireless captive of the hearth. But a nature composed of such huge rhythms is universal, not rooted and recognised in only one small spot. So Kathleen Behan, passionate socialist and Fenian, born in the 1880s, and mother of a hectically competing brood of Republicans and writers (Brendan, Dominic, and Brian among them), is far more than an Irish *mater familias*. She is all the matriarchs, from Jewish to Italian, whose long experience of dazzling cheerfulness, unquenchable grief and caring spills over into everything.

Kathleen, who died in 1984 at the age of 95, became the subject of the distinguished actress Rosaleen Linehan's one-woman show, *Mother of All The Behans*, which ran both in Dublin and at the Edinburgh Festival in 1989. An affectionate, humorous, and sometimes elegiac portrayal which, through soliloquy, evoked the boisterous, gossipy nature of working-class Dublin itself, the piece was drawn from Brian Behan's biography of his mother's bold and tender life and was dramatised by theatre director Peter Sheridan.

In the way that O'Casey's characters were the very blood and guts of Dublin itself, so too was Kathleen Behan's story that of the city incarnate; a vivid, unrepentant voyage – from orphanage to terminal nursing home – of a bright, strong chatterer who married twice and raised her children only to see all but one of the seven emigrate.

'But sure what would keep them here? Only idleness,' she reflected. Here was not a romantic freedom-fighter breaking loose of privilege to support the poor, but a realist who understood that the price of nationhood would mean another brand of violating hardship.

Rosaleen Linehan never met Kathleen Behan but she came to the role with an immediate understanding of its period mood and setting as a result of her own parents' legacy of piquant Dublin anecdotes. 'It's a piece of work I find desperately moving because Kathleen was such a human and generous spirit. She might have been a bit boring when drunk, singing 40 songs too many, but try as I did I couldn't find a single person who had anything mean to say about her.' Kathleen Behan didn't, in fact, sample alcohol until she was 62, but there are those in Dublin who will tell you admiringly that once embarked, Ma Behan was no slouch in raising the old glass. 'I've heard it said,' confides Linehan, 'that she could down ten whiskeys in a night and not even bat an eye.'

In terms of her own career Rosaleen Linehan is something of an impressive late starter herself – at least in the context of dramatic gravitas. Up to seven years ago she was regarded exclusively in Ireland as a musical review and comedy artist, drawing a huge and loving audience throughout the country. Even so she allocated only three months of the year to work; the rest of the time was devoted to her children, three boys and a girl, and her husband, the journalist and author of much of her cabaret material, Fergus Linehan.

However, once the children were launched on adulthood, Linehan decided quite methodically to kill off the old jokey image and embark all over again on the cruel road to auditions, challenging directors to cast her in difficult and serious parts. Playwrights like Brian Friel, Frank McGuinness, Jennifer Johnston and Tom

Murphy, knowing her immense versatility, encouraged the switch with offers of characters from their own new works. Then came the classics: Chekhov's *The Seagull*, Shaw's *Heartbreak House*, O'Casey's *Plough and the Stars* and Shakespeare's *Twelfth Night* in which Linehan gave a mesmeric performance as Feste, the clown, lowering her agile voice to that of a man's and wearing, throughout Joe Dowling's stunning production at Dublin's Gate Theatre, a shabby frock coat, corkscrew trousers, spats and decrepit hat. The whole appearance evoked an ashen melancholy – somewhere between Beckett and Chaplin – and it is to Linehan's great credit that many of those in the audience who read the theatre programme only on their way home never realised this wise little broken-down jester was being played by a woman. 'I was truly delighted when I heard that because the last thing I wanted to give was a camp performance,' she says. 'With great courage Joe Dowling left it to me to interpret the character but, honestly, up to four days before we opened I was still adrift. I knew I wanted Feste to be a small, odd sad figure going around with the fellas but at the heel of the hunt all the same. And then suddenly it clicked. As the production was set in the Twenties I physically built him into an amalgam of those early film comedians: Stan Laurel, Harry Langdon, George Robey and a tinge of Chaplin.'

Any doubts that Linehan might not master the risky thrills of drama were finally demolished after that appearance, and now with international awards buttressing her reputation, she is easily recognised as one of Ireland's leading actors. Her recent performance in both London and Dublin of the Friel play, *Dancing at Lughnasa*, has been acclaimed by many theatrical critics as the highlight of each city's season. 'My poor husband keeps saying: "Not another indomitable Irishwoman – could you not play Rita Hayworth next?"' Not yet at any rate, for *Lughnasa* was now destined for Broadway.

Occasionally, though, the fans from those early, pithy Dublin successes approach her in the street and say: 'Ah, Rosaleen, yer not going to stick with that ould Chekhov stuff, are ye?' But Linehan has never had any intention of retreating and just as many others stop her to ask when she's thinking of taking up Shakespeare again. 'I'd love to do much more of it,' she muses. 'But my age is probably against me. Shakespeare didn't go in for many middle-aged women.' Yet who knows? Having accomplished Feste so magnificently Rosaleen Linehan might just be headstrong and inventive enough to pitch her extraordinary talent towards the ultimate adventure – a woman playing Lear.

8

CITY, STATE AND CHURCH
St Patrick and St Peter

FOR CATHOLICS it was not the second coming but the first. The leader whom they had loved for centuries had swooped down from the sky at last, and as an airport breeze ruffled the plain white robes into baroque sculpture John Paul II knelt and kissed the ground. So began the historic and most extraordinary journey of the Bishop of Rome to Ireland. Ireland semper fidelis, always faithful.

Days before that breakfast-time arrival in Dublin most of the country's three million people had been on the move, travelling mainly by foot or by specially routed public transport to their nearest vantage point to greet the Pope. Not since his first Papal visit home to Poland would John Paul raise the staff of peace over so many heads, hug so many children or press so many hands. Mother Ireland of the sagas was a pilgrim once more, simultaneously stepping forward to claim a sophisticated world's attention, and back again into the ancient litanies of binding faith. That weekend, of 29 September 1979, not only marked the nation's greatest honour, it also etched its dual identity: a culture climbing the rockface of discovery between old isolationism and new, heady recruitment to the European bloc.

Dublin's sacred kitsch merchants were out in force, of course, hustling Papal souvenirs ranging from rugs bearing the Pope's face to iced cakes shaped like open bibles, or gaudy interpretations of Dürer's praying hands. At the religious counter in Clery's department store those queueing for small, collapsible chairs, to carry to

John Paul's Mass in Phoenix Park, grew restive. 'There's no use demanding what I haven't got,' warned an agitated sales assistant. 'The fact is there isn't a single Papal stool left in the whole of Dublin.'

Dublin's intelligentsia were hardly enthusiastic, however. In an age forlornly lacking leaders John Paul II was emerging not only as one of the most compelling figures of our time but as a man hewn from granite and that most paradoxical of things, a reactionary who was popular, an unyielding disciplinarian who was loved. With justification the liberal wing believed that the rigid Irish hierarchy was using this visit to put the brakes on progressive thinking. And certainly many of the pulpit calls had rung with the kind of Redemptorist scolding which many modern Catholics found irrelevant. In the cause of spiritual renewal some clerics had advocated a sort of floating Lent, urging the faithful to abandon cigarettes, alcohol and sweets in preparation for the Papal tour. 'They'll be asking us to give up sex next,' announced a Dublin bus conductor to his lower deck. And sure enough, one passenger had read a letter in the Irish Press from a man in Clondalkin insisting that 'we all revert to the pre-Norman custom of sexual abstinence before major religious festivals'.

But in other ways requests for soul-searching hit home. Dr Enda McDonagh, one of the Republic's most respected scholars, pleaded that all churches recognise their 'share in the blame' for the monstrous violence in the North. And feminist concern over the Papal visit found unstinting support in the writer Anthony Cronin. At a packed public meeting in Dublin he spoke of John Paul's devotion to the Virgin Mary, a pledge which in Ireland had often been used to make women resigned to their lot as unequal citizens.

Ultimately, though, much was expected of the Pope on that exuberantly merry weekend: that he should excommunicate the IRA; that he should halt strikes, unite Christians, improve the telephone service, inspire a spiritual and intellectual revival, and miraculously stop the spread of litter. In short, that he be all things to all people.

Since then, and in the last decade particularly, two inescapable perceptions have motivated the drive towards a more secular Ireland, and both are born of disobliging facts. Firstly, the close integration of Church and State in Dublin has exacerbated the divisions between the North and South. Dr Noel Browne, one of the Republic's foremost radical thinkers and a revolutionary Minister for Health between 1948 and 1951, argues persuasively that in ensuring Ireland's principal loyalty was to Rome before the State, Eamon de Valera encouraged the emergence of an arrogant, triumphalist and ultra-montane brand of Catholicism in the South. 'Under de Valera's influence Irish republicanism was literally turned inside out,' he has written. 'It became anti-democratic, xenophobic, philistine, anti-intellectual, and opposed to secularism, pluralism and socialism.' And inevitably the net result of this concentration of the South's Catholic soul was the intensification of the Protestant soul in the North.

The second secular impulse revolves around the Republic's own growing perception of itself as a European country. Perhaps more than any Western nation Ireland is culturally in transit between old ideology and new. Here now is another influential (and individually more prosperous) faith called Common Marketry. Dublin has always had its corners of opulent style, its pampering restaurants and élitist clubs, but its international swagger today is more liberally spread. Young graduates emigrate not just to the predictable market places of London, Boston and New York, but to Paris, Brussels, Amsterdam or Frankfurt. The bourgeoisie, with its January-to-January suntan, has created Irish holiday enclaves along much of Spain's Costa del Sol, and all this integration with somewhere else has caused Dublin to wear its European outlook confidently, as if it were donning some showy international overcoat. Rising living standards, higher economic expectations and the growth of consumerism have been among the fruits of EC membership for Ireland, and it may be that the intoxicating pleasures of materialism have more to do with the drive towards a secular republic than any real increase in tolerance for other religions.

As mentioned elsewhere here a recent study by the Maynooth Jesuit and sociologist, the Rev. Micheal MacGreil, illustrated that from a random sample of 1,000 people only 52 per cent of respondents (94 per cent of whom were Catholic) would marry a Presbyterian or welcome a Presbyterian as a family member; only 40 per cent a Jew, and only 31 per cent an agnostic. But while Ireland remains a more obviously and deeply spiritual country than many others, falling church attendances suggest that it has not escaped the processes of secularisation seen everywhere in Europe, except, perhaps, in Poland. Dr MacGreil's study also shows that attendance at weekly worship is still remarkably high (82 per cent), even though there has been some falling away. In 1974 a comparable survey revealed a 91 per cent turnout for devotions. Ten years later it was down to 87 per cent. The latest figures show, too, that Mass attendance (between 1988 and 1989) was lowest in Dublin city and Dublin county. But although the decrease, in MacGreil's view, is not substantial, the Republic's birth rate – for many years in excess of European standards – is at last falling. Thus, the Church's army would appear not just to be in retreat but in perceptible decline. The Jesuit notes that the intensity of parental commitment in handing on religious beliefs to children has also diminished since the early 1970s, indicating 'a possible reduction in the status of religion in the home or in the school'.

Dr Garret FitzGerald, of Fine Gael, was that rarest of the Republic's Taoiseachs: a leader who risked his own political career in the cause of creating a more secular Irish society. He was among the few politicians who openly acknowledged that the excessive influence of the hierarchy was an obstacle to a united Ireland because it gave the South a sectarian quality that was rebarbative to other denominations. In 1981, during a radio interview where he used the phrase a 'Republican crusade' – later translated into 'Garret's crusade' – he denounced the direction the State had taken. In particular, he said, it had betrayed the principles of Wolfe Tone (1763–1798), a founder member of the Society of United Irishmen which aimed to break the connection with England and unite 'Protestant, Catholic and Dissenter in the common name of Irishmen'. Because he spoke as Taoiseach, FitzGerald's words outraged many. But they arose from a continuing battle to roll back the Church's influence in Irish life, a battle which thunders along to this day on the key issues of social policy such as contraception and divorce. Thomas McCarthy, the poet who recently published his first novel set around the wheeling and dealing of Fianna Fail workers, argues strenuously that although religion is also central to the Fianna Fail experience, it means little to the party. 'It's really like a traffic accident, something to be avoided at all costs,' he observed in an *Irish Times* interview. 'The people, or most of the people who founded Fianna Fail, have been excommunicated. The Church Triumphant is Fine Gael; Fianna Fail doesn't have the need for a line to God through the hierarchy – instead their line of power is populist.'

Dr FitzGerald may have retired from the fray after the defeat of the divorce referendum in 1986, but the forces of change for which he fought cannot permanently be frustrated if Ireland is to conform to European social norms. However, the profundity of the change required of the Irish system cannot be disguised. The 1922 Constitution with which Britain set up the Free State was secular in spirit. In fact the Catholic Church was not even mentioned yet politicians immediately sought an alliance with the Church, which became part of the new conservative establishment. Because of its overwhelming following, it was seen by almost all politicians as the cement that would bind the nation together. With moving eloquence Noel Browne has reflected in a series of lectures that the South, totally inexperienced in the exercise of power in a popular democracy, slid 'willingly into the secure, welcoming anti-democratic totalitarian cocoon' of Rome's imperialist rule: 'The effect of this, as a child, I saw in my own home. As with so many poor peasant families of our class . . . both my parents, while literate, had been taught little except a blind, unquestioning faith in Rome, and an uncomplaining subservience. Protest against even the most heartbreaking experiences was called "flying in the face of God" and was forbidden . . . They believed in a set of steps which were prepared for them, and by which they could escape Hell and gain Heaven. Fear of Hell, and an angry God, motivated their lives and determined their behaviour. For the cynically wealthy few in power, to this day, it has been a useful discipline over many.'

The approval of the Church became a weapon in the struggle between W.T. Cosgrave, leader of the first Cumman nan Gaedhael Government, and de Valera's anti-Treaty Republicans who had been excommunicated during the Civil War. After the foundation of Fianna Fail in 1926, de Valera sought to outflank Cosgrave in the bid for clerical support and favour, and the Church welcomed these advances. The late Tod Andrews, quoted by the journalist John Cooney in his book *The Crozier and the Dail*, wrote of 'the lengths to which the Church would go to maintain its dominance of a peasant population steeped in superstition and an urban proletariat soused in Saint Joseph's medals, Saint Blaise's flannel and a dozen different varieties of scapulars'. At that period the Papacy was centralist and authoritarian. The First Vatican Council's response to the Church's receding temporal power had been to enunciate the doctrine of Papal infallibility, and for the Vatican, the Romanised Irish Church, with its fidelity and conservatism, were good deeds in a naughty world. It was able to exploit its influence in the infant state to acquire a leading role in the development and delivery of social policies, applying the principles of the 1931 Papal Encyclical *Quadragesima Anno* which put forward the idea of 'subsidiary function'. This doctrine saw the state's role as greatly circumscribed. It would oversee the provision of services, but it would not itself deliver them. This would be left to vocational organisations. And moral policy was a matter not for the State but for individuals guided, of course, by the teaching of the Church.

So the Republic in the early days took little account of its hero Daniel O'Connell's concept of a free church in a free state. John Cooney wrote: 'Increasingly the barque of St Patrick was tied to the barque of St Peter which claimed the exclusive right to issue administrative orders to the crew.' The Vatican had, in the early Twenties, rejected ecumenism, finding validity in it only as a means of restoring separated brethren to the true Faith. The Irish Church enthusiastically applied this doctrine and through its alliance with politicians was able to imprint into the political system the idea that the Church had a duty to ensure that legislation should direct men and women to live a moral life in a society permeated by Catholic values. Partition had placed three-quarters of the Protestant population in Northern Ireland and only one in ten of the Republic's population was Protestant by 1926: in the Republic then the Church's dominance encountered no serious challenge.

There was great unhappiness, however, among those remaining Protestants, about the impact of policies developed out of the tight partnership between Church and State. The *Ne Temere* decree on mixed marriages remained in force until as recently as 1970, when it was modified. And before the Free State emerged, Protestants who could afford to do so were able to evade the absence of divorce courts in Ireland by petitioning Westminster. Attempts to carry this right into the new State were rejected by the Dail in 1925. Protestant voices were raised in anger for here was perceived a breach of their civil liberties and a first sign that they would not receive fair play. In an emotional speech to the Senate, which his Catholic colleagues found offensive, W. B. Yeats described the need to unite North and South as the 'deepest political passion' and warned that the North would not give up any liberty which she already possessed. 'If you show that this country, Southern Ireland, is going to be governed by Catholic ideas and Catholic ideas alone, you will never get the North. You will create an impassable barrier between South and North . . . you will put a wedge in the midst of the nation.' Adding a powerful plea for Irish Protestants, of whom he was, of course, one he declared they were one of the 'great stocks of Europe'. They were the people of Burke, Grattan, Swift, Emmet and Parnell, individuals who had created most of the modern literature of the country, the best of its political intelligence.

Despite Yeats's hopes that the Protestant tradition would reassert itself within the Republic, the Catholicisation of the Free State went ahead rapidly. Protestants Need Not Apply became the not uncommon official line in Southern Ireland, and although many Catholic citizens did detest the sneering discrimination of such clauses Noel Browne recalls that in 1930 President de Valera was confidently able to justify the sacking in Mayo of a properly appointed and highly qualified librarian because she was a Protestant. He intoned: 'I say the people of Mayo, a county where I think 98 per cent of the population is Catholic, are justified in insisting on a Catholic librarian.' By 1923 film censorship was introduced. In 1924 laws sought to curtail the consumption of strong drink, at the prompting of the bishops. By 1929 the Censorship Board was in place. Dr John Whyte, in *Church and State in Modern Ireland, 1923–79,* noted that the process of enshrining the Catholic moral code in the law of the State continued at the same vigorous speed under the Fianna Fail Governments headed by de Valera from 1932 onwards, culminating in the passage of the 1937 Constitution. Dr Whyte wrote: 'Mr Cosgrave refused to legalise divorce; Mr de Valera made it unconstitutional. Mr Cosgrave's Government regulated films and books; Mr de Valera's regulated dance halls. Mr Cosgrave's Government forbade propaganda for the sale of contraceptives; Mr de Valera's banned their sale or import. In all this they had the support of the third party in Irish politics, the Labour Party. The Catholic populace gave no hint of protest. The Protestant minority acquiesced. The only real opposition came from a coterie of literary men whose impact on public opinion was slight.'

These forces were formally acknowledged in de Valera's 1932 Constitution, which recognised the 'special position' of the Catholic Church. He sought and received Papal approval for it. Indeed Pope Pius XII regarded it as a model, with a large measure of social policy derived from Papal Encyclicals.

The challenge to the pre-eminence of the Church came from several sources of which the Protestant community was perhaps the least influential. The Church itself was moving away from its anti-materialist position as leading churchmen began to recognise the need for material progress. However, they insisted that it had to be within the framework of Catholic social and moral teaching. But economic stagnation, after the the Second World War, began to destroy the idea that the State should play an auxiliary or subsidiary role and the battles between Church and State, which were to be so marked an aspect of post-war Irish politics, were already emerging. In the Forties, the Commission on Vocational Organisation had attacked the State's incompetence which was traced to the exercise of power without accountability by civil servants. But matters came more spectacularly to a head in 1948 with the crisis over the Mother and Child Scheme planned by Dr Browne, then a young and enterprising Minister for Health in the coalition Government formed that year. In the context of the welfare policies developing in Britain and elsewhere in Europe, Browne's proposals were unexceptionable, even timid though as much as could be expected in a relatively poor country without a large industrial base. Mothers would get free health care from GPs and hospitals. The claims of the Church were spelled out in the attack launched on them by the Bishop of Ferns, Dr Staunton. 'The right to provide for the health of children belongs to parents, not to the State. The State has the right to intervene only in a subsidiary capacity, to supplement, not to supplant,' a reassertion of the doctrine in the pre-war Encyclicals. Dr Browne was quickly abandoned and forced to resign, and in a scathing report to London the British Ambassador noted that since a major part of the hierarchy's objections to the scheme had been the absence of a means test, the bishops were encountering the highly unusual phenomenon of public odium.

It was a classic instance of Church influence. Dr Whyte, analysing the involvement of the bishops in legislation between 1923 and 1965, lists only 16 statutes out of 1,800 measures but suspects their influence was more widely pervasive. In 1953 the bishops were able after a meeting with the Government to secure virtually all the amendments they sought to the compromise Health Bill. The coalition could hardly have been more intimate, and the Act spoke eloquently of the hierarchy's political muscle. But the impact on British opinion was unfavourable. The declaration of the Republic in 1948 had already prompted Westminster to pass the Ireland Act guaranteeing the Northern Unionists their status in the UK. It is a matter for speculation how much the Northern Government's blatantly discriminatory policies against Catholics were, indeed, encouraged by the Catholicisation of the Republic itself.

The quick butchery of Dr Browne's proposals must have encouraged the Church to think its dominance was untroubled. But in the Republic it would never be a glad, confident morning again: the civil service, appalled by Ireland's economic backwardness after the war, was fighting back. In the Fifties it was to lead the rush for growth, and political voices were emerging to challenge the Church's claims to determine social policy and moral choices. Among the leaders of the reforming troops were Dr FitzGerald and the young Senator Mary Robinson. Under the leadership of Sean Lemass and Terence O'Neill, the South and the North did achieve some measure of rapprochement, although that tender element was to be put under enormous strain in the Sixties by the eruption of the Troubles. In 1972 the Constitution was amended, a referendum having approved the removal of the reference to the Church's special position, and the lowering of the voting age.

Since then Irish politics have been characterised by a series of conflicts about social policy in which the Church, increasingly defensive and not invariably successful, has sought to resist liberalising legislation. Leading churchmen have largely abandoned the idea that the State should play second fiddle, and have been prepared to concede its role as legislator. But most of them have continued to insist that the legislation should reflect the Church's social and moral teaching.

The persistent struggles over contraception do much to explain the Church's uneasiness about leaving law to the lawmakers. Its anxiety to some extent arises from the fact that in the Irish Constitution the Supreme Court is able through its decisions to mould social policy. Attempts to change the law on contraception had been made by Senator Robinson and others in 1971 but their Bill was unsuccessful. However, they forced the Government into a promise that it would prepare its own legislation. It was evident by now that the hierarchy's root-and-branch opposition to contraception was out of step with popular habit and opinion. The 1935 law had forbidden the sale, manufacture or importation of contraceptives but by 1974 doctors estimated that 35,000 women were taking the pill and the Irish Family Planning Association was providing contraceptives and advice. Initiated in Dublin but taken up throughout the country, the Women's Liberation Movement orchestrated a spectacular campaign, travelling from Belfast to Dublin on the 'contraceptive train' from which supporters flourished the condoms they had bought in the North. The Church shifted its position. The hierarchy issued a statement conceding the right of legislators to determine the question, though with the familiar caveat that they had to take account of the impact on the 'quality of life' in the Republic.

At this point the intervention of the Supreme Court threw matters into muddle with a judgment that was to have the result of making churchmen permanently nervous about entrusting Ireland to the parliamentary process. Instead they sought to write in to the Constitution mechanisms to bind both courts and legislators. This was a response to the famous McGee judgment in which the Court held that parts of the 1935 Act were unconstitutional, throwing the law into muddle and opening the door to the widespread legal use of contraception, which obviously gave enormous encouragement to the women's movement and other groups fighting for more liberal social policies. Mrs Mary McGee was the mother of four children, living in a mobile home near Skerries, County Dublin. On health grounds her doctor had advised her she should have no more children and she was fitted with a diaphragm which was to be used along with spermicidal jelly, a small supply of which was given to her by the doctor. When the supply was finished, she applied by post to England for more. The package was seized by Customs under the Act but the Court found that those parts of the law which forbade citizens to import contraceptives for personal use were unconstitutional. It also determined that family planning rested with the couple alone, and the couple's right to make an unimpeded decision was protected by the Constitution. The net effect of the judgment, as Charles Haughey was to remark in 1979, was that there was no longer any control over the importation of contraceptives and that it was now legal for anybody, irrespective of age or marital status, to import them provided they were not subsequently to be sold.

In 1974 Mrs Robinson tried again with a modified Bill. Again the Government responded with the promise of its own legislation.

This proposed that contraceptives could be imported and sold under licence by chemists; only married couples were to have access. Widows and widowers were regarded as unmarried and fines of up to £500 would be imposed on those convicted of breaking the law. Sensationally, the Government's Bill was defeated when the then Taoiseach, Liam Cosgrave (the son of W. T.), led six Fine Gael deputies into the opposition lobby. Matters rested in some confusion until 1979 when during Mr Lynch's third administration, Mr Haughey, as Minister of Health, introduced his Family Planning Act, which made the supply of contraceptives dependent on a doctor being satisfied that they were for 'bona fide' family planning purposes. It had all the characteristics of a compromise and gave to Irish political history a phrase which inadvertently pointed up the nationalistic lunacy of the whole situation. It was, said Mr Haughey, 'an Irish solution to an Irish problem'. He had trodden the middle ground and in attempting to please everyone he pleased few, despite his insistence that the plans would meet the wishes of the great majority of 'sensible, responsible citizens'. But he got the Bill through the Dail.

Judges interpret the law but all Supreme Courts are political. In the US, the Supreme Court had, under the influence of jurists like Mr Justice Brennan, played a significant part in liberalising policies on segregation and it had ruled in favour of a woman's right to abortion on the general grounds that the Constitution protected the rights of individuals. The permissive society was everywhere celebrated and the women's movement was rampant in the US and Britain. For some clerical observers in Ireland the Supreme Court was showing disquieting liberalising tendencies also. The McGee case then had one other lasting consequence: it signified the end of the Church's snug alliance with the legislators by demonstrating that, even if the politicians toed the line, the judges might not.

In 1983, with Dr FitzGerald installed as Taoiseach, the Bishop of Kerry, Dr Kevin McNamara, launched a crusade against abortion, illegal in Ireland since 1861 though it was estimated at the time that about 3,500 women a year were travelling to Britain to end their pregnancies. His campaign used shrewdly alarmist techniques that were to become standard in later battles with the State on such matters as divorce. These were to suggest that one social change would open the floodgates to more, and in the context of this rhetoric, contraception would lead to promiscuity, divorce to the general abandonment of marriage and abortion to wholesale infanticide. Indeed, Dr McNamara, as he stomped the country, asked whether the 'slaughter' of unborn children would become an accepted part of Irish life. The campaign's objective was a pre-emptive strike against any legislation that might permit abortion. The Irish people were asked to give their verdict on the eighth amendment to the Constitution, inserting a clause acknowledging the right to life of the unborn and guaranteeing laws to defend it. The measure was seen by its critics, who included Dr FitzGerald and Senator Robinson, as at best equivocal and at worst sectarian. In the event the amendment was endorsed by a two-to-one majority, though some interesting conclusions were drawn from the vote. For a start, the turnout was low, at about 53 per cent. But the result also threw into prominence the growing divergence between Dublin, with its more cosmopolitan and sophisticated attitudes, and the rest of the country. In the city, there was a much narrower margin, and Dick Walsh wrote in the *Irish Times* that this reflected new and deep divisions between urban and rural sections of the electorate, with urban, largely middle-class areas providing strongest resistance to the amendment and predominantly rural constituencies voting 'Yes' by majorities up to 4 or 5 to one.

To this day Garret FitzGerald smarts at the memory of that defeat and with some justification he maintains that the result was merely a Pyrrhic victory for the right-wing as 50 per cent of the electorate didn't bother to vote at all. John Cooney asked: 'Was it the "last hurrah" of a certain type of Catholicism?' Dr FitzGerald had opposed the amendment but had not cam-paigned against it, an equivocal position which did him little good in the country, but he had not given up the fight against Church interference. Indeed, he had spent much time, as Foreign Minister, in explaining to the Vatican why a pluralistic society was both inevitable and desirable. When Dr McNamara was appointed Bishop of Dublin in 1984, he paid an early official visit to Dr FitzGerald at Government Buildings. Next day the Bill to liberalise contraceptives was to be published. The Taoiseach, on the grounds that it was a State matter, not only failed to seek the Archbishop's advice, he did not even warn him of the Bill's publica-tion. So the battle had been rejoined with the result that – as John Cooney observed – the Irish State, for the first time since its foundation in 1922, had defeated the hierarchy in a trial of strength with an elected Government over a matter of public morality. The Dail passed the Bill by a narrow majority but it was enough to allow Dr FitzGerald to claim that the vote asserted the authority of the State against any kind of outside pressure. It was a modest enough victory for the Bill proposed that condoms and spermicides should be available without a prescription to people aged 18 and over. Within an hour of its publication, Dr McNamara had denounced it in characteristic terms, with the warning that it would lead to a litany of sinful afflictions: premarital sex, moral decline, venereal disease, teenage pregnancies, illegitimate births and abortions. Mr Haughey predictably weighed in on the Bishop's side and Dr FitzGerald was faced with the alliance that had so often been successful in the past – the hierarchy, Fianna Fail, parish priests and recalcitrant lay pressure groups. Intense pressure was put on deputies. The Bill was eventually carried, despite the defection of three Fine Gael deputies, with the help of two members of the Workers Party and an Independent. Mr Desmond O'Malley, who had already lost the Fianna Fail whip because of his principled public departure from the Haughey line on a united Ireland, warned the Dail that a defeat of the Bill would gladden Unionists in the North and extreme Catholics in the Republic. He reasserted the Republican tradition's aim of reconciling Catholic, Protestant and Dissenter; and he helped the Bill's passage by absenting himself from the Dail. For this he was expelled from Fianna Fail and went on to form the Progressive Democrats, a tiny party without whose support his old foe Mr Haughey could not have formed his administration in 1989.

But the triumph was not decisive. Dr FitzGerald encountered damaging grassroots hostility and the Church fought back with its successful opposition to his proposals to legalise divorce. This rejection of the divorce referendum in 1986 preceded Fine Gael's loss of power which marked the end of that period in which Garret FitzGerald, first as Foreign Minister and then as Taoiseach, had campaigned to remove some of the barriers within the State to any prospect of reconciliation with the North. He came to grief, yet that phase is still remembered as an honourable attempt to change the esteem of one sort of Irishman for another. But the root cause of the divorce referendum's failure lay in an ancient terror: the loss of property and land. Fianna Fail saw divorce as the means to unhinge FitzGerald's Government and roar back to power. With a cynicism seldom equalled in modern European politics it exploited the Church's standard opposition by waging an outrageous scare campaign which left many women particularly in a vice of utter fear that divorce was a way to evict them from their homes. However, the alarm-mongering wasn't exclusively Fianna Fail's. Alice Glenn, one of Fine Gael's own deputies, announced that: 'Any woman voting for divorce would be like a turkey voting for Christmas.'

But the fact is that in the North, where divorce is available, the rate of marital breakdown is lower than in the South. Mary Harney, joint-founder with O'Malley of the Progressive Democrats and Minister of State with responsibility for the environment, points out the illogicality of the entire position: 'If you take Armagh, on the border,' she says, 'divorce is obtainable in the north part of the diocese but not in the southern part. Yet in the context of a united Ireland some churchmen have argued that divorce would be recognised but until then we couldn't have it in the Republic.'

The arguments against sectarianism as an obstacle to political progress in the North remain a strand in the continuing debate. When the word pluralism is used in this context it has an extensive sub-text for it is the code name for the abandonment of sectarianism in the fabric of the State. But even more significant are the social and political forces at work in loosening the grip of the Church. Dublin has not escaped the scourge of drugs and drug abuse is a classic death route for the spread of the AIDS virus, immune to pulpit preaching. The incidence of the disease in the UK has been contained by the homosexual community, which has moderated its habits of promiscuity, but the virus is now travelling, in the UK, through heterosexual elements which have not. It is a curious postscript to three-quarters of a century of Church domination that, now it is receding, the need has never been more evident for high standards of personal morality if only to inhibit the growth of a terrible illness, and, for the same reason, a pragmatic attitude to social policy. The permissive society has run its tawdry course and marriage and fidelity are back in fashion. But the arguments for the widespread availability of condoms, or free needles for drug abusers, have never been more powerful. That does not of course mean that the marital and familial bonds demanded and imposed by the Church since 1922 cannot survive in the Europe of 1992 where divorce is available everywhere save in Ireland; but it implies a personal morality consistent with much Christian teaching.

The European movement, unless it falters because of the strains thrown up by German unification, is likely to go much further than the harmonisation of the marketplace after 1992 or the convergence of economies. Mr Haughey has argued, convincingly, that the development of European unity will eventually moderate the conflict between North and South by making it meaningless in the context of an integrated political and economic institution. What is sauce for the goose is sauce for the gander, and the same argument applies also to social policy. That is the new reality with which legislators and Churchmen alike must deal.

As for the Church, its grip on power in the first place arose from its ability to influence the electorate. It is now reviewing its own declining attendances and the implications of the falling birth-rate and some Churchmen have argued that its privileged position in Ireland has been bad for it by making it distant and unresponsive. Certainly it remains an élite at the top, and its reluctance to change was demonstrated by an early failure to implement the decisions of the Second Vatican Council for partnership with the laity. Yet it is impossible to imagine this land of 'saints and scholars' without its Church, but its future importance and influence will depend on whether it can retain its hold on the minds and affections, and attendance, of the masses.

Recent years, in fact, have witnessed the emergence of a new left-wing tendency in the Church, directed by those priests and nuns in religious orders who have become radicalised by their mission experience among the poor and politically oppressed in Central and Latin America and the Philippines. According to Father David Regan, a Holy Ghost priest who worked in Brazil, the young Irish laity are already marching – away from the church doors – in protest. 'A profound national rethink of what we are about as a Church, of where we are going and how we propose to get there, would still appeal to many – especially if they were invited to participate.' It is easy, too, in any broad critique of the battalions of St Patrick and St Peter to overlook that very impressive and solid layer of caring, spirituality and compassion with which the humble working Church has sustained Irish society, often through its greatest sufferings. The priority given to family life, with its respect and attentiveness towards the elderly, is very much a Catholic characteristic, as, indeed, it is in Mediterranean countries.

Most priests, in the view of Brian Lenihan, a former Deputy

Prime Minister, are not over-concerned with theological matters: 'Ours is a very pastoral, social Church,' he says, 'because the Irish themselves are that sort of people.' And, of course, no one should under-estimate the Irish gift of irreverence, the nod-and-wink subversion that is born from an instinctive dislike of authority. 'The electorate won't wear authority stamping on it in any way,' reflects Lenihan. 'So that means a politician, priest or policeman – any of these sort of people – must exercise power with circum-spection. They can't rough up the Irish electorate. It's a very subtle relationship.'

Much of Paul Durcan's fiendishly compressed wit and icono-clasm as a poet is derived from his rejection of Catholic puritanism, and it is a signal of how much times have changed that the work of this Dublin writer is among poetry's best-sellers. His *Irish Hierarchy Bans Colour Photography* jabs a sharp, satirical finger into bull-necked intolerance:

> *After a Spring meeting in their nineteenth-century fastness at Maynooth*
> *The Irish Hierarchy has issued a total ban on the practice of colour photography . . .*
> *The general public, however, is expected to pay no heed to the ban;*
> *Only politicians and time-servers are likely to pay the required lip-service;*
> *But the operative noun is lip: there will be no hand or foot service.*
> *And next year Ireland is expected to become*
> *The EEC's largest money-spender in colour photography.*

With hindsight it may be that the Papal visit of 1979 provided only an artificial buttress to the outward strength of Catholic authority in matters of sexual and public behaviour. As he was to do some two years years later in Scotland, the Pope chose his words about Ireland brilliantly, acknowledging the sense of isolation it had often felt, 'situated on the remote edge of Europe'. And in that acknowledgement he recognised the loneliness and heroism of its early Christians, but there were also plenty of explicit warnings against social permissiveness, and the message about spiritual and moral discipline could not have been more clear. Everywhere – from Dublin's Phoenix Park to Galway – the words were received with ecstatic cheers. Yet not even the priests who hear the sins of the people can be entirely sure if Ireland is still *semper fidelis*, for in this, the last decade of the the 20th century, that old gravitational pull towards the confessional is also in decline.

FATHER BERNARD TREACY, a Dominican priest in Dublin and the editor of the Irish monthly journal, *Doctrine and Life*, spoke about the need for the Church to be aware and supportive of certain shifts in society: 'These days the opposition to legal changes on divorce, or contraception, may well be fighting a losing battle. Many of us, in fact, were very unhappy about the tone of the divorce referendum in 1986 and I think that, but for a very peculiar combination of forces at the time, it would have been carried. Indeed, I'm not sure that the Church's opposition to the proposed constitutional change was as effective as it might have seemed. Fianna Fail was particularly determined to damage Garret FitzGerald politically on that issue and to that end the party summoned up a very atavistic thing – the fear of losing land, a fear which goes back to the Famine, and the Land League. It was as potent a force in people's rejection of divorce as any declaration by preachers. And it was drummed up more by lay groups and politicians than by the official Church. What was used was the argument that if divorce occurs, then you could find yourself having to sell the family home and no roof over your head. Even where it is not rural, Ireland retains a strong sense of rural values, and a strong feeling for the land.

'But, you know, there is no longer, if there ever was, a single homogeneous clergy. Attitudes among us vary quite a bit. That's why people shop around for confessors but then I think they always did. In a way, I suppose, the Irish clergy is very much like the Italian; there is a sense that you must deal with people *simpatico*. Possibly the Irish are similar to Italians in other ways too. There is a wonderful play by Brian Friel called *Translations*, and in it an English lieutenant asks an Irish schoolmaster why he doesn't teach English to his pupils, and he replies – I'm paraphrasing of course – that the Irish have a natural affinity with the people of the Mediterranean. That's why he teaches Latin and Greek, he says.

'I think, though, that by and large people have become more secular, and less likely and quick to interpret events in a religious fashion. In some ways that is good, but in others it is detrimental if there is a growing unwillingness to value a spiritual component

to people's lives. That is clearly an impoverishment. Yet if secularisation means a jettisoning of superstition, that could actually be
a reaffirmation of religious consciousness. A purifying which
allows religious sensibility to be more truly religious, freed of superstition about relics and the like. These things can be explained in
an intellectual way, but one doubts whether the actual use of relics
accords with the intellectual explanation. But the moving statue
phenomenon at Ballinspittle, a few summers ago, and similar
events were very intense examples of what seems to be happening
to the psyche of the Irish people. There is a quest for spirituality
which appears not to be met in today's world. The fact that people
went to watch religious statues, in the hope of seeing them move,
indicates they are searching for some kind of experience. Others
look to charismatic prayer or meditation groups. And within the
parishes which have the greatest deprivation it seems to me that
both community life and church life are often very alive. There have
been quite inspired appointments of parish priests in some of these
areas, priests who have created very much a people's parish,
encouraging self-help and a community spirit. Now, with church
guidance in many cases, the travelling people are also beginning to
assert their identity, seeking a sense of self-worth.

'But in other instances you have people going to church out of
habit, people who nevertheless possess a very low level of belief,
and that I think is a considerable worry. There is always a temptation for priests to want a tightly organised church made up of
people who are sort of manageable. But if it is to be a people of
God rather than an army, the Church has to be composed of people
of varying dispositions and of varying levels of commitment. So the
temptation to want it to be rigidly organised, full of individuals who
don't break rules, that temptation, I think, has to be resisted. But
with recent falls in the number attending church, there is a need for
creative and imaginative pastoral approaches, a need for much
more imaginative preaching. One way to do that would be the
preparation of sermons in conjunction with people. That would
avoid the old thing of a priest "doing a de Valera", looking into
his heart and expounding on people's needs through his own
expectations of them. I wouldn't want people to begin dropping
away from church-going if they don't feel perfectly committed.
The doubter may give the priest more trouble but there is an
integrity there. Some time ago there was an interesting little piece

of information thrown up by research, which showed that among those in Ireland who describe themselves as convinced atheists, 12 per cent believed in the devil. Which suggests that being a convinced atheist is . . . God knows what. Perhaps a kind of drifting. You know, taking some things loosely from the religious atmosphere into which you were born, and declaring a non-interest in other things.

'I think that one of the saddest aspects of both the abortion debate and the divorce referendum in this country was the way in which people who were doing careful thinking on the issues felt they were being deliberately isolated from the Church. These weren't amoral individuals. Personally they might have the greatest difficulty in advocating divorce or accepting abortion, but after much conscientious deliberation they had come to the decision that people might have the right to a law which tolerated their availability in certain situations. Yet Sunday after Sunday from the pulpit they were being told that there was no room for debate. There was a great deal of damage done by that. Good, thinking, caring people were made to feel excluded from the Church. That should never happen again. Priests have very definitely no right to tell people how to vote. Our job is only to clarify the issues.

'Do priests sometimes feel troubled and helpless over the killings in Northern Ireland? I think in the South priests are conscious of the need for delicacy – people from the South can trample on the feelings of Northerners very bluntly, and they are also conscious that in our own Troubles here in 1916–22 a lot of clerical denunciation went very much into deaf ears and within five years of that denunciation the bishops were appearing on platforms with the very people they had denounced. So there is some memory of the ambiguities that can arise. But at the same time it is very, very troubling that the warnings against something as clearly wicked as the killing of innocent people are simply being ignored by the perpetrators. There is the genocide of Protestant farmers in Fermanagh. It is quite clear what the IRA have been doing there. It's an appalling affront. And no matter how priests speak out, their words are not heeded. So, yes there is great pain.

'Because of his condemnation of violence the late Tomas O'Fiaich was, on occasions, a man in personal danger from one side or the other. There are many stories of mysterious cars following him. Priests in Dublin would not be in such a precarious position.

But there are people in the city who place themselves at risk because they are not scared to express their horror at what is happening in the North. At the offices of *An Phoblacht*, the Sinn Fein newspaper, you will not infrequently see people picketing in protest. One morning – it must have happened very early when no one was about – their doorway was covered with cow's blood. Before the next IRA atrocity, someone had made the kind of prophetic gesture which takes courage. I am unhappy to hear killers in the North described as psychopaths. They are murderers. To call them psychopaths is to allow them a medical excuse.'

9

SCENES
Bewley's

SOME YEARS AGO a little woman was in Bewley's in West-moreland Street, hammering into a grandiose éclair, when she suddenly declared: 'Isn't it savage to think that a place like this is always in danger of closing down? Soon there won't be an institution left in the whole of Dublin where a body can kick off the old shoes and enjoy a cup of tea without being done an injustice.' At the time the hatchet of ruthless accounting was about to fall on Bewley's but then, almost during the last hour before execution, a takeover bid by Campbells, the caterers, saved the café chain from extinction. Yet in that woman's regret there you have it – the universal lament for disappearing shrines, and the natural infuriation people feel about being turned into exiles on their home ground.

Six years on Bewley's has undergone refurbishment. Nothing too drastic, of course, or else Dublin's garrulous hostility would have probably caused the shutters to fall in the decisive way that those earlier accountants had intended. And anyway Bewley's distinction has always revolved around a kind of cosy fatigue; a stuffy warmth that wafts over you rather like the fusty heat in a hurtling old railway carriage locked against the cold. From the beginning it was one of those sanctuaries which excelled in being classless: the genteel matron, lips pinched in *sotto voce* gossip, felt as welcome there as the schoolteacher or the man of commerce huddled down behind his hangover and *Irish Independent*. Bewley's was special, many vacant hours being spent on its dusty red and brown

upholstery, shafts of light glinting down from Harry Clarke's luscious stained-glass windows in Grafton Street, and the chat taking on that seductive anecdotal roll which Dublin seems to have invented as a means of communication between strangers.

In Bewley's heyday (which even now seems to be the period of every generation's first strut into adulthood) you could stand outside Trinity College, waiting for the bus to Dalkey, and the nutty aroma of finely ground beans, travelling on the wind from Westmoreland Street or down to the same spot from the café on Grafton Street, would whip up the nostrils and clean out the sinuses, invariably enticing you to forget bus timetables and head instead in the direction of matured Java and perhaps an almond ring. In its 150 years Bewley's has given much of Dublin a softly inebriating whiff of the exotic. And yet not too much, for Bewley's has always been careful to balance the unknown with the familiar, serving barm brack alongside strudel, or offering the improbable pleasure of Irish stew washed down with Lapsang Souchong.

There are coffee and tea shops all over western Europe which are similar in concept but hardly any match Bewley's raffish air. Maybe this is something to do with the fact that Bewley's is like a club for Dublin's lifelong bachelors who frequent it from the unmade bed of their dismal digs seeking the solace of home cooking. In Paris, Rome and London such places have a bone-china refinement. In New York they resound with the agitated cries of noisy professionals doing business. But in Dublin the talk, as in the pubs, flies off on philosophical tangents encouraging circular conversation which can be hijacked by anyone. Try to nail it and you toil in vain, for the essence of Dublin chatter is fluid, contradictory, oblique: 'And why wouldn't I vote a feminist into the Presidency of Ireland?' says a man who has been spooning his soup to the sound of his own diatribe against the women's movement. 'Sure, isn't it a job where the incumbent has to be nothing but neutral, so that alone will shut Mary Robinson up for a good few years.'

Long ago, pre-decimalisation, an aunt found herself in Bewley's sitting next to a pair of holy marys, the kind of elderly Dublin women who always have a prayer on their tongue and outraged respectability in their eyes. At the time a young but dead Latin-American member of the clergy, Martin de Porres, was in the process of canonisation and the faithful, anxious to speed up the Vatican in this matter, were using his saintly memory like a clothes peg from which to hang their novenas. Anyway, this particular day in Bewley's one holy mary says to the other: 'Amn't I just coming from the religious counter in Clery's where I wanted to buy a statue of the blessed Martin, and the girl hands me down this one the colour of soot? So I says to her: "Mother of God, I never knew he was as dark as that. Do you not having anything lighter?" And she says to me: "That's the colour he comes in for 17s 6d. They do a paler one for 25 shillings but it won't be in until Tuesday." Well, I tell her that I can't wait that long. Haven't I got to get the novena going before then? So I bought the 17s 6d model. But would you ever take a look at it, Kitty! Isn't he very black for a priest?'

But if Bewley's has been saved from the bulldozer, much of Dublin's old corners of great style have been shamelessly ransacked to make way for crude office blocks and those other concrete structures which always signify that the greed of speculation has got the upper hand. Now, at last, there is a determined effort to save what Georgian grace is left. However the conservationist instinct has not sprung from the politicians. Instead it has come from a dogged band of once derided protectionists whose valiant efforts have now coincided with impressive outside examples from cities like Glasgow which have set to and mended the fabric of their finer days.

Dublin, in its role as one of the European Community capitals, has also been embarrassed into cleaning up and securing its past architectural masterpieces if only to silence the influential dismay of so many visiting diplomats at embassy parties. (That said, the American Embassy itself is an eye-sore, dating from the 1960s school of concrete brutalism.) And there is EC money now to clear away some of the ugliness of urban decay, but it remains a scandal how much of the poorer north side of the city has been left to rot while much of the south side, with its droves of affluent and articulate householders, offers handsome evidence of unstinting architectural caretaking.

Walk along Eccles Street from the Mater Hospital towards the faded neo-classical grandeur of St George's Church on Temple Street and on the right you pass a terrace whose Georgian grace has been gouged out by neglect. Yet it could still be saved not necessarily for the benefit of what in Dublin passes for yuppiedom but as decent, renovated housing for the people who belong to these streets. Cries that such schemes are impractical carry little conviction today, especially in the light of Glasgow's achievement. Against a history of some of the worst slums in Europe, this Scottish city has made an impressive start in bringing home-dwellers of modest means back into the heart of the town. Today they live there in small but well-equipped modern flats whose Edwardian and Victorian facades have been preserved and washed to revive the original sandstone glow. The physical horror of the Gorbals was demolished long ago, but dumping its incumbents in bleak, peripheral housing estates is now recognised as an act of unwitting betrayal. Yet for decades the social wisdom of maintaining inner housing stock has been ignored at hideous cost. Deprived neighbourhoods, like those around Dublin's Gardiner Street and Sean MacDermott Street, spiral downwards into violence, becoming voluntary no-go areas for everybody else. And thus their problems produce the stuff of cultural apartheid where the stains of poverty are matched by thugs' rule and the plundering materialism of racketeers.

Eccles Street is at the core of Joyce Country – what the author described as 'blotchy, brown brick houses'. There is no trace there today of Number Seven, the address of Joyce's Leopold Bloom, which now lies demolished and buried beneath the private hospital wing of the Mater. But for a while the author himself lived off the North Circular Road, at Number 17 North Richmond Street, and there is much in *Dubliners* which describes the neighbourhood exactly: 'The houses of the street, conscious of the decent lives within them, gazed at one another with brown imperturbable faces.' But in small, self-contained ways some ambitious gentrification is emerging in Dublin. Off O'Connell Street the market traders' turf of Moore Street is now as lively with red and green awnings and 'period' shop fronts as it is with the cracked-voiced banter which shoots back and forth across the stalls: 'Ah, missus, would you put away that dirty fiver and give us something cleaner?' says a vegetable seller to an intimidated customer who immediately obeys. As the woman walks away, the stallholder warns her next purchaser: 'I'm telling you, you could catch mad cow's disease from the filthy money that's going about these days.'

Francis Street, once a badly scarred limb running through the old working-class area of the Liberties, today provides an example of the curious urban proximity of shabbiness and wealth. At the top end the Iveagh Market remains with its drab little jumble stalls

selling dead men's clothes, broken picture frames and inconsequential lumber. Then, as the street winds down towards the
Church of Ireland cathedral of St Patrick's, the junk shops turn
into antiques boutiques, and drinking shops are transformed into
recherché credit-card restaurants and theme saloons. St Patrick's
was, of course, the platform of one of the greatest rebels of them
all, Jonathan Swift, who was Dean of the cathedral from 1713 to
1745, and in that time he preached with eloquent ferocity against
British oppression.

In a corner off the nave Swift's imposing black leather chair
stands near the pulpit from which his mighty oratory raged. He is
buried close to the cathedral's entrance, next to the grave of Esther
Johnson, his 'beloved Stella', but whether the couple ever married
remains one of those mysteries lost deep in the cathedral's stones.
'Here lies the body of Jonathan Swift, where fierce indignation can
no longer rend the heart.' This is Swift's own epitaph although the
cathedral also records the more overblown version by Yeats: 'Swift
has sailed into his rest; savage indignation there cannot lacerate his
breast.' Flanking the Dean's memorial plaque, today, there is a
counter selling fund-raising bric-à-brac, some of it demurely folksy
like the Celtic cross candles but other pieces provide a refreshing
hint of barrowland amid the cloistered calm. It's a scandalous
thought but the kiss-me-I'm-Irish keyrings look as if they might
have fallen off the back of a passing horse and cart from John
Street.

Outside, in St Patrick's Close, Marsh's Library confirms that in
Dublin literature is never far away. This enchanting and often overlooked little gem of learning was the first public library in Ireland
and one of the earliest in the British Isles. It was built in 1701 by
Archbishop Narcissus Marsh to a design by Sir William Robinson
who had previously been the architect of the now exquisitely
restored Royal Hospital building at Kilmainham. Today Marsh's
Library remains a magnificent example of a scholar's paradise with
its burnished oak bookcases featuring carved and lettered gables
crowned with mitres. Liturgical works are here in profusion, but
so too are rare titles on medicine and law, science, travel, mathe-
matics and navigation, all relating to the 16th, 17th and early 18th
centuries. In 1705 Archbishop Marsh acquired his most valuable
collection from the estate of Edward Stillingfleet, Bishop of
Worcester. For this he paid £2500, an indication of his own private

fortune, and the 10,000 books purchased then include some by the earliest English printers: Berthelet, Daye, Fawkes, Notary, Siberch and Wynkyn de Worde.

But Narcissus knew that even the most cultured individuals could succumb to temptation, and to prevent the theft of his precious books he chained many to the shelves and also installed within one of the library rooms three wire cages, rather like confessionals, inside which readers were locked while they studied the most valuable texts. When their study was completed they rang a hand bell to summon a keeper with the key, and since they derived such pleasure and insight from the written word it presumably didn't matter much if their 'jailer' was a dilatory fellow with his own head lost in a book. Much of the library's excellence today depends on the love and commitment of its custodian Muriel McCarthy, the only woman to be appointed to that post by Marsh's governing body. Hers is an amateur's devotion in the best meaning of that phrase. Since the library exists on funding of little more than £10,000 a year she is virtually the library's unpaid scholar in residence. But Muriel McCarthy's knowledge and obvious delight in books make her unforgettable to those visitors from around the world who, driven by inquisitiveness to explore the bend in the road behind St Patrick's, chance upon Marsh's doorway set in the stone wall protecting its secret garden. Since 1988, as the result of a substantial private donation from an American couple in New York, the Delmas Conservation Bindery has been operating at the library, giving a healthy, lively appearance to both leather-bound and vellum-covered books. Marking Dublin's year as European City of Culture Marsh's mounted a fascinating exhibition drawn from its own early manuscripts from those countries now integrated in the EC. In *And Then There Were Twelve*, the catalogue to the display, Muriel McCarthy and her co-author, Ruth Whelan, dismiss any notion that the library is an intellectual fossil. 'To browse among these books,' they write, 'is to explore a hidden world vibrant with curiosity which has been one of the hallmarks of Europe's cultural heritage'. Marsh's Library, they note, is a treasury of what might be called the European mind.

Out on College Street, towards the Bank of Ireland, there is a traffic island dignified by a statue of the lyrical maestro Thomas Moore. During the summer a busker from another age positions herself at his feet, placing her baggage at such a crafty angle that

Moore's cocked finger seems to be commanding bystanders to direct any loose change straight into her collecting tray. She stretches and squeezes traditional airs and jigs from her accordion with a kind of solid, unchanging delivery which suggests she is operated by clockwork. The smiling head moves from side to side in the same mechanical manner and, apart from the reckless addition of a Caribbean sunhat, she dresses entirely in the colours of the Irish flag. Set against the dishevelment of nomadic sax-players and catarrhal Dylan-esque chanters this busker appears like one of those old folk dolls you find in duty-free shops. Yet she has clearly had her moments for propped inside the lid of her little brown case there are dozens of pictures of her posing with celebrities, including former President Ronald Reagan. As for Thomas Moore, the landmark urinal he stands beside has now been padlocked into redundancy. A disappointment, really, given that Moore was the man who composed *The Meeting of the Waters*.

Just as the spirit of James Joyce is everywhere in Dublin so the ghost of Brendan Behan seems to be forever holding forth over a pint of foamy stout. In life Mulligan's of Poolbeg Street was one of the writer's favourite haunts and although Behan died in 1964 the pub remains true to his taste for un-*chic* decor. In this bar the rough wooden tables look as if they could be the same ones that furnished the place when John Mulligan founded it in 1782. It was here that Behan would meet one of his Dublin friends who always claimed to be on drinking terms with the novelist Evelyn Waugh – a surname he would pronounce as Warr. 'She was a tough woman,' the friend would say. 'A great soldier and a great warrior. She was called Evelyn because that was her name, and she was called Warr because she was all for war.' Well, fair enough.

10

THEMES
Censorship

LITERARY EXILES – from Joyce and Beckett through to Brian Moore, John McGahern and Edna O'Brien – are among the traditional itinerants of Irish history; artists who have felt their creative spirit so under threat from the petty sneers and pressures of locality that survival required emigration. Subsequently, of course, many have made their reputations by writing powerfully, if obsessively, about that complicated land they left behind.

'It is the country I know best,' reflects O'Brien in explaining such preoccupation. 'Fervid, enclosed and catastrophic. As Hemingway said, when you are writing about a room, you must know it, even if you don't want to describe it . . .' To outsiders it is a baffling irony indeed that Dublin, so endowed with cosmic writers, should have felt righteously obliged to send many of them packing. Even today the Republic retains its censors' list of books which are deemed unfit for common purchase – the result of a law passed in 1929 – although the likes of Joyce, Beckett and O'Brien are no longer included. In truth the list now is generally perceived among booksellers and public alike to be nothing more than a meaningless anachronism. Nevertheless there are times when the Censorship of Publications Board, as if excavated from a state of comatose indifference, lunges in the direction of some hapless author and ostensibly flattens his sales potential with the full blast of its outraged tone.

Inexplicably, Dr Alex Comfort's now standard textbook, *The Joy of Sex*, was among titles to be banned in the late 1980s. After much protest the order was revoked in 1989, but the book had in fact been prohibited in Ireland since its publication in the early Seventies. In normal circumstances orders cease to have effect after 12 years but in the Comfort Case the ban was promptly renewed in 1987 amid vigorous cries from the various liberal lobbies in Dublin who argued persuasively that the Censorship Board was utterly out of touch with modern Ireland and its international aspirations.

Meanwhile the pub panjandrums of the city stoked the derisive muttering over pints with claims that the Board was making a jackass of the country, and also let fly the playful notion that this was probably all part of a large-scale Government plan to ban sex altogether and thus provide a peculiarly Irish solution to AIDS, birth control and – while we're at it, lads – any perilous economic crisis round the corner. The fact is, however, that the rules of censorship in Ireland, as with so much of the nation's legal framework, are applied with a nod and a wink.

Like the Italians, the Irish incline quite naturally towards a form of intimate anarchy: a sort of inborn compulsion to beat the system. More than anything this flouting of authority seems to stem from the collective heritage of nimbly circumventing the dictates of overlords and priests. A woman in the process of parking her car on a double-yellow line near Trinity College in Dublin is suddenly aware of a guard noticing her efforts. Quick, he tells her, pull the motor in tight over the yellow and the warden mightn't notice. But for all its jovial instances, this selective blindness helped for generations to obscure any true understanding or appreciation of free thought and free speech. In post-colonial Ireland, the old, departed enemy was in effect replaced by a brand of soft totalitarianism, a coalition of rigidly conservative politicians and brimstone clerics whose power depended on a specially tailored morality and ideological vision of Ireland which saw sex and dissent as the greatest sins, and demanded society's unquestioning obedience.

In pursuit of this isolationist dream Dublin, for all its native waggery and tangential satire, became inward-looking and repressive, its culture ruled by smug mediocrity and philistine conventions, and the kind of subservience which gorges on the belief that the less disturbance caused, the better. 'The Dubliner is of the mounteback race, the most useless and inconsistent,' said James Joyce, and certainly there was no reason why the novelist should have remembered the city of his birth with any great pleasure, for all through his writing life Dublin turned a dismissive back on him for the savage brilliance with which he exposed its verbose and ineffective loungers and the scurrilous element in its soul.

'It's an ill bird that fouls its own nest,' wrote Sir John Mahaffy of Trinity College in 1927. 'James Joyce is a living argument in defence of my contention that it was a mistake to establish a separate university for the aborigines of this island – for the corner boys who spit into the Liffey.' Seventeen years on Dr John Charles McQuaid, Archbishop of Dublin, could match the vehemence of Mahaffy's sentiment but in the opposite direction: 'No Catholic may enter the Protestant university of Trinity College without the previous permission of the Ordinary of the Diocese. Any Catholic who disobeys this law is guilty of mortal sin and while he persists in disobedience is unworthy to receive the Sacraments.'

Yet despite the poisoning conformity and the viciousness of so many personal reminiscences James Joyce never lost an affection for Dublin. He loved its wicked pith and bitter hilarity, its woeful vulnerability and desperation. In *Joyce: The Man, the Work, the Reputation*, Marvin Magalaner and Richard M. Kain recall that when Con Curran, a friend of Joyce, would ask the author when he was returning to Dublin, the reply invariably was: 'Have I ever left it?' *Ulysses* was published in Paris by Sylvia Beach in 1922 and after reading it George Bernard Shaw, by then living in England, wrote :'To me it is all hideously real. I have walked those streets and known those shops and heard and taken part in those conversations, and 40 years later, have learned from the books of Mr Joyce that Dublin is still what it was, and young men are still drivelling in slack-jawed blackguardism just as they were in 1870.'

For many of the best writers who have followed, Joyce's genius imposed a kind of petrified self-censorship. The novelist and film maker, Neil Jordan describes that sensation now with a clarity which springs from true escape: 'I grew up near Dollymount Strand in Dublin which wasn't very different from what Joyce portrays in *Dubliners*. Like him, I hung on to my imagination as the only redemption in this grey, paralysed culture. *Portrait of The Artist as a Young Man* could be my story. And that's the problem. It articulated my condition as a budding writer in my late teens so well that the act of writing for myself seemed redundant.'

Jordan did write to acclaim, however. But after his anthology of short stories, *Night in Tunisia*, and his novel, *The Dream of a Beast*, he abandoned creative writing.'I did my best to avoid this literary Tower of Pisa collapsing on top of me. I located my stories in landscapes which Joyce had not described, such as little seaside towns north of Dublin. I tried to address themes which were different from his.' Every writer, Jordan maintains, must devise his own strategems to avoid the crippling influence of Joyce, the colossus of 20th-century fiction. 'My ultimate strategem was to start writing films instead.'

A sharp insight into the severity of censorship imposed in Ireland can be seen in the recent publication of State papers from the years between 1922 and 1960. Such was the volume of banned films in 1930, for instance, that the Cinematographers Renters Society warned that it would not have enough movies to keep its halls in business. The one-piece bathing suit – 'Or what is known as the university costume as used in swimming and diving competitions' – was the main target of the censor John Montgomery's wrath. Mr Montgomery, in his custodial role, objected to its appearance in what was described in an unintentional play on words as 'the rising tide of unsuitable films', and, despite the cinematographers' plea to the Minister of Justice, he appears to have rushed for the scissors at any glimpse of semi-nudity or the vision of revue girls with bare legs. There was a paradox here, of course, in that such delights were permitted in the theatre, but for the puritanical Mr Montgomery even the sight of female gymnasts required punitive editing. Defending his zealous commitment to public decency he insisted that he did not deal as drastically with films as many would have wished. 'I don't cut bathing or diving, but I do cut exhibitions of beauty parades where men are seen pawing girls in bathing suits – vetting them – as it is elegantly described – and close-ups which are obviously pandering to exhibitionism . . . A strong stand should be made in the interests of common decency whatever the conse-quences.' Neither could the stock characters and incidents of 'movieland' escape Mr Montgomery's scrutiny by adopting Holly-wood's evasive circumlocutions: 'A rape will not be called an erotic impulse, a paramour will not hide behind the euphemism of lover or sugar-daddy, and I certainly will not wrap a piece of tawdry tinsel around a prostitute or mistress and call her a gold-digger.'

Literary censorship at the time not only proclaimed much of Joyce obscene. It also predictably proscribed Lawrence's *Lady*

Chatterley's Lover as well as Aldous Huxley's *Brave New World* and Liam O'Flaherty's *The Puritan*, each described as indecent. Even publications like *Nursing Mirror* and *Midwife's Journal* were banned because they contained advertisements for contraception. However quaint and amusing such rulings seem now, their collective effect on the Irish psyche was debilitating; stifling creative talent at home, and reinforcing both squalid prejudices and hypocrisy.

Fear of running foul of censorship bred a craven mentality in sections of the media. In 1930 the manager of Dublin's *Independent* newspaper compromised that journal's very title by asking the Minister of Justice for his opinion on a full-page advertisement for Twilfit Corsets. 'Although we do not see anything in the advertisement to render it unsuitable for publication,' he wrote, 'it occurred to us that some of our readers might take exception to its appearance.' The official reply was pompously benign: the Minister would not consider it necessary to direct the institution of criminal proceedings should the advertisement be inserted.

As international studies on censorship confirm, the effect of such cultural insularity on both the artist and the public causes a kind of intellectual decay. Wounded by being denied an audience for his work, the writer very often suffers a further harassment of the worst kind of provincialism. The persecution inflicted on the widely respected novelist John McGahern after the banning of *The Dark* in Ireland in 1965 has been well chronicled, but even by the narrow standards of the day the action was extreme. Condemned by the censorship board as obscene, *The Dark* was McGahern's second novel and the scandal heaped unjustifiably on its title not only cost him his job as a primary school teacher but also forced him out of Dublin.

Since he had to make a living, London offered the immediate alternative but even over such a short distance the difference in cultures was more of a chasm than a gap: London, careless and pulsing with the hedonism of Sixties liberation, and Dublin, despite all its convivial swagger and outrageous wit, still muzzled by the warped flesh-lashing diktats of an admonitory élite. 'A poisonous crowd,' remarked Samuel Beckett. But McGahern's confidence had been so shaken by the whole affair that he wrote nothing further for three or four years.

In *Banned in Ireland*, an extensive study on censorship and Irish writers, edited by Julia Carlson, McGahern wonders now whether that creative block might not have happened anyway. But he does recall that the 'unpleasant thing about both the banning and the sacking was that . . . it brought something prurient into it, which for me had nothing to do with whether a work is good or bad.' Similarly, Edna O'Brien tells Carlson: 'One gets very confused . . . by accusations. If people tell you you've written dirt, even if you know you haven't, some of it stays with you. I wanted to go away very far. Australia even.'

Today books by McGahern and O'Brien are easily available in the bookshops of Dublin and elsewhere. Indeed for McGahern, who now lives on a farm in County Leitrim, fate's wheel went into a total reverse spin with the publication of his scrupulously observed and quietly sorrowful book, *Amongst Women*, which in 1990 won the Irish Times/Aer Lingus Irish Literature Prize for Fiction, and also that year was shortlisted for the 1990 Booker Prize in Britain. But in relation to his earlier shameful treatment he remains a man without bitterness, explaining Ireland's anti-intellectualism, to Carlson, more as an aberration than a fixed condition: 'It was a young insecure State without any tradition, without any manners, and there was this notion that to be Irish was good . . . there was this whole mentality that if you could build this fascist, blue-blood Irish race and that if everybody learned Irish and knew no English, that all foreign corruption influences would be kept out. I think censorship was a kind of by-product of that mentality.'

More than 15 years have passed since the Censorship Board banned a book by an Irish writer. Indeed in the matter of censorship now the unenforced law seems to be the thing. Everyone in Dublin knows that a list of forbidden books exists but hardly anyone, including booksellers, can tell you which books are proscribed. If pushed, people might recall the *Joy of Sex* rumpus, although the book cast out originally because of its bondage section is now widely on sale. Or they might mention that to be caught reading Joyce's *Ulysses* must surely once have been considered a mortal sin. In fact the Censorship Board never ostracised *Ulysses* despite Molly Bloom's scalding monologue on sex. But then it didn't have to as initially hardly any of Joyce's major books were made available to Ireland.

Not all that far from Leopold Bloom's shabby but enticing

territory in Ulysses you will find Number 13 Lower Hatch Street in Dublin, a house of fallen Georgian grandeur where the original magnificence can just be glimpsed beneath the institutional paintwork of a civil service building. Here Oifig Chinsireacht Fhoilseachan, the Censorship of Publications Office, piquantly shares an address with the Criminal Injuries Compensation Tribunal. The juxtaposition couldn't be more Joycean, leading the visitor almost to expect an encounter in the hallway with those young men full of useless jabber and cunning. Instead you meet the congenial Peggy Garvey who runs the Censorship Office and scorns authoritarian dressing for black lace stockings and stilettos.

In effect she sits waiting for offending books to be submitted by the public and, she is happy to say, her postbag is diminishing. Growing enlightenment isn't the only reason for this: in Dublin, as in every major city, the video market is overtaking book sales. Although serious literature can still be banned in Ireland – unlike in any other European country – Garvey believes censorship should continue as a means of excluding pornographic material, a view actively supported by feminist organisations. Books regarded as indecent or obscene reside in an under-the-counter limbo for 12 years unless their prohibition is revoked by the Appeals Board before that length of time. Those books which advocate abortion are on the list forever and inevitably include works by the birth control pioneer Marie Stopes.

Simone de Beauvoir's *The Second Sex* is on the list, as is *An Outline for Boys and Girls*, edited by Scotland's Naomi Mitchison. And, more unaccountably, Barbara Cartland's *Marriage for Moderns* is also on the index. To date scarcely a dozen serious fictional works remain banned. Gore Vidal's *The City and the Pillar* and Erica Jong's *Fear of Flying* have been reprieved, along with *Onward Virgin Soldiers* by Leslie Thomas. But Anaïs Nin's *Delta of Venus* still lodges on the list and, totally improbably, so does Guy de Maupassant's *The Colonel's Nieces*.

The third section of the register is mostly concerned with sleaze magazines but, overall, the impression is of random censorship rather than systematic draconian strictures. If Gore Vidal was once there why not John Updike? If sexologist Nancy Friday has been targeted why not that other socio-voyeur Shere Hite? The answer could be as simple as this: the five official censors, drawn from different aspects of Irish life and including a judge, are already extremely preoccupied people. They are appointed by the Minister of Justice but the business of weeding out the pernicious, although time-consuming, is purely an honorary task. And if two censors agree a book should not be banned, then it escapes the hatchet.

One other fact which makes the list so arbitrary is that each complaint must come from the public and be accompanied by a written explanation, plus a copy of the unacceptable work. That last stipulation takes a lot of steam out of a grudge for books are not cheap nowadays and, anyway, the average busybody doesn't want to be spotted handing over money in a shop for a dirty title. Meanwhile much that is still illicit will find a loophole by way of an old trick once employed by the playwright Hugh Leonard. Obliging friends overseas would parcel up consignments of forbidden works and dispatch them to his Dublin address, filling in the customs form as follows: *Sender – Sister Mary Aloysius. Contents – religious tracts.*

11

CITY, STATE AND CHURCH
Garret FitzGerald

GARRET AND CHARLIE. Rarely has the Irish political scene been sharpened by such opposing forces: the first an intellectual with an international reputation for brilliance and a liberal stance; the second, long secured in folklore as a buccaneer and born-again survivor. Given the dubious doings and the power-driven notions that have encircled Charles James Haughey over the years it is curious that Garret FitzGerald, during his 25 years as a Fine Gael Deputy, did not wrest the Taoiseach's crown more often from the Fianna Fail leader. But FitzGerald's lack of fighter's chutzpah – the very absence of which endeared him to the public – was also his surest handicap in the grimy world of power politics.

Charlie and Garret. Garret and Charlie. In a country of just more than three million, half of whom are under the age of 25, it seems almost an affectation to call politicians by their full names. And, besides, the primitive realism of Mick the Begrudger has not entirely disappeared from Irish life. Assume familiar terms with the great and you can presume to keep them at your level. Should they fall into the trap of believing themselves something special then the gaudy friendliness turns nasty. Garret FitzGerald retired from active politics in 1987 after 25 years during which time he had gained considerable respect abroad both as Irish Foreign Minister from 1973 to 1977 and as Taoiseach from June 1981 to March 1982 and then again from December 1982 to March 1987. Throughout much of the latter years deep-rooted hostilities between him and

111

Charles Haughey were hardly concealed but while Haughey's personal credibility with the public frequently plummeted, FitzGerald's sometimes soared but never dropped to the same humiliating degree.

But the Irish electorate is essentially an enigmatic creature. What people say to politicians is not necessarily at all the way they will vote. Such inscrutability may be among the legacies of colonialism, a conditioning born of centuries of foreign rule, but the Dubliner, especially, tends to answer questions obliquely applying an almost oriental sense of camouflage. Further afield what this elusiveness meant to Garret FitzGerald, he insisted, was that at least ten per cent of the West of Ireland vote (traditionally Fianna Fail's staunchest territory) represented closet Fine Gaelers. 'Our research has consistently shown this in the past,' he said in 1982, 'but not one of these voters will ever tell a canvasser that they are going to vote Fine Gael for fear of jeopardising long-standing Fianna Fail benefits to rural communities.'

To some extent that explanation defined one cobwebby aspect of Irish politics. British-style class politics with candidates reduced to labels are utterly alien to the Republic. In Ireland people vote for the candidates they know because he or she is a neighbour or a cousin or a national name. They vote for the man or woman who gets things done for them rather than for an ideological ticket.

Or so it seemed until the General Election campaign of February 1982 when FitzGerald set himself the Olympian task of giving Ireland its first modern election. The Troubles in the North were scarcely mentioned. Indeed, for the first time in years that tragic landscape became irrelevant to the enemy without – the men in grey suits from the IMF. FitzGerald fought the election on the country's crucial economic issues only, leaving Haughey looking incongruous with his old glad-handing techniques. And the crusade almost worked. The finer points of economic strategies filtered right through society. So much so that when two Fianna Fail canvassers arrived on the Glasnevin doorstep of one senior citizen and, misunderstanding her grasp of world affairs, promised to see that her gutters and windows would be fixed if she gave them her vote, she replied sternly that she wasn't interested if it meant 'more foreign borrowing'. Yet Garret FitzGerald lost that election by the narrowest of margins because, it seems, the electorate couldn't stomach his draconian budget proposals.

By 1986, FitzGerald had instituted the divorce referendum in his dogged campaign for constitutional change, a crusade through which he hoped to make the South seem more amenable to the North. His opponents, though, were quick to see this as a device to distract the electorate from his 'penny-pinching measures'. Such vigorous dismissal ignored a genuinely urgent desire for change on issues like contraception and marital collapse. But the Government's campaign was poorly conceived and ill prepared for the alarmism spread by FitzGerald's attackers, who claimed that any 'such tinkering' with the marriage laws would leave women virtually penurious. This was Fianna Fail fielding all its dirty tricks to play on confused anxieties and primal fears. And it worked. So, within three years, two brave referenda had been lost in FitzGerald's attempt to nudge Ireland towards a modern social democracy. The result of the first had enshrined the illegality of abortion in the Constitution by a vote of two to one. Dissent about both episodes can still be heard in all manner of places. To this day Garret FitzGerald smarts at the memory of his defeat and maintains that the result in the abortion referendum was merely a Pyrrhic victory for the right wing as 50 per cent of the electorate didn't bother to vote.

With Mrs Thatcher, FitzGerald was a signatory of the Anglo-Irish Agreement at Hillsborough on 15 November 1985. But, in fact, long before that there had never been any doubt about his determination to seek Common Ground with the Six Counties. To that end he worked with that most tenacious and articulate of Northern politicians, John Hume, along with Dick Spring, FitzGerald's coalition deputy, and an inevitably obstructive Charles Haughey, to devise the New Ireland Forum, a political initiative that aimed to bring together any strands of hope that might be woven together into a new solution to the lacerating tribalism that had come close to maiming an entire island. In Dublin the eagerly awaited and painstaking document was recieved so enthusiastically that no one was quite prepared for Mrs Thatcher's contemptous dismissal of its three suggested alternative goals – unification, confederation, or a joint body to administer the Province. 'Out . . . out . . . out,' she snapped at a press conference following a November summit in 1984. Such confrontational rudeness was not only an insult but a signal that the British Prime Minister had little comprehension of her Irish counterpart's own acutely sensitive position.

FitzGerald's commitment to a united Ireland stems directly from his family background – a Southern Catholic father and a Northern Presbyterian mother – and this makes it impossible for him to believe either that Ireland is two separate nations or that it is one with a uniform culture and religion.

Was he too nice to be an effective Prime Minister? His old sparring partner Conor Cruise O'Brien has observed: 'He is about as nice as you can be and get ahead in politics, but no nicer. There is steel under all that pretty wool.' At 65 Garret FitzGerald is now 'free' from daily politics and in a position where he can speak or write about causes that interest him. A united Europe, something to which he has always adhered, stands high on that list, as he stressed during our interview: 'Membership of the EC has been of very substantial economic benefit to Ireland whereas the economic benefits for Britain have been less clear-cut. It is also a fact that our relationship with the outside world in the first half century of independence was very much dominated by Britain (for the first 35 years or so we were moving through various stages to complete separation, starting as a self-governing dominion in the Commonwealth, moving to sovereignty). So the question of disentanglement from Britain was also a major factor in making us pro-European. While we had disentangled the political relationship, with independence, we were still tied to Britain very closely in economic and monetary terms, and the EC offered a way of reducing that dependency. At one point after the War 93 per cent of our exports were going to Britain. By the time we joined the EC it was about 68 per cent, and now it is around 31 per cent. And while Irish exports to the EC were very small indeed, they are now nearly 40 per cent. Also monetary independence from Britain has helped us economically and psychologically. Ordinary people participated in the debate about Europe before the referendum and when they came to take the decision it was based on very full information about the issues. The poll itself showed 83 per cent in favour of the EC on a 70 per cent turnout, so that positively settled the matter. Even those who were against the Community decided that although they didn't like the idea, they would make the best of it. Having said that, there are still some concerns, but they are much less than you might think because we haven't any sense of losing our identity.

'The hangups which were a consequence of the historic relationship between Britain and Ireland have become much less, and although Northern Ireland is a continuing cause of tension between us we have largely been successful in creating structures to contain the remaining problems and deal with them in conjunction with Britain.

'But as to how the average person in the South regards Northern Ireland, it is much less important to them than it really is: I mean there is always a tendency here to underestimate its importance – to turn away from it and to want nothing to do with it. Not among the politicians: on the whole they have faced up to it and given it a priority much greater than public opinion wants or likes. In terms of popular support the Anglo-Irish Agreement turned out all right, but in the run-up to it the decision by me and others to spend so much time and energy on Northern Ireland was widely disapproved of by the public. This is largely because of the general distaste for violence and bigotry; this breeds the feeling of not wanting anything to do with it, therefore stay away. And there is also a feeling that if you just forget it, it will go away. It won't bother us. There's an introversion here, and a certain selfishness of attitude, but given the threat of violence it is understandable. It's a human reaction.

'Losing the referendum on divorce was a blow but I'm philosophical by nature. I felt it better to have a referendum and even lose than not have it at all because at the time it was becoming a major issue in public opinion. It was liable to overflow into a General Election and it didn't seem sensible that in a country with major economic and financial problems and worries about the North we should fight an election about divorce. There is a variation of self-criticism here and it's called begrudgery. In fact it isn't self-criticism at all but a way of criticising those around you. It is a very negative thing and there is a tendency towards it in Dublin. Perhaps it's a feature of a small country, but on the other hand we have applied self-criticism in two key areas in the last 20 years and the result has required some fairly fundamental rethinking of inherited attitudes. First our nationalism has changed from "Give us back our Six Counties" to the realisation that re-unification can come only with the consent of the majority in Northern Ireland. That's a total reversal of opinion – moving from an inherited position which was ill thought out and negative in its effects to a positive one arrived at rationally by standing back and seeing the dangers of that sort of exaggerated view of ourselves.

' And second, the matter of sovereignty: we don't attach the same significance to parliamentary sovereignty as the British do and it has been far less of a problem for us. There is an outside perception of us as an emotional people, but, in fact, we have acted very rationally on the subject of Europe, whereas the British, it seems to me, have not, at any stage, faced up to the fact of Europe and how British interests can best be secured in a Europe which is united. To be half way in and half out out, you are bound to lose. There's been a dithering about since the end of the War, and this has been very damaging to Britain. It's a curious thing – which the British would rarely acknowledge – but we've acted far more rationally than they have. Yet our history has made us rational. People who have had trouble acquiring the ownership of their land tend to be very hard-headed. On this island we don't apply the word peasant to small farmers but if you think of that word in a European context, well, you think of hard-headed individuals, not very emotional but very clear where their interests lie. That is true of our farming population also. But I do think there are few countries that on two very fundamental issues have in fact reversed inherited emotional attitudes to take a rational position in argument. It is very unusual to do that in a space of 20 years.

'In any country, if the capital has as large a population as Dublin has (30 per cent of the population), then the relationship between the capital and the rest of the country can be somewhat complicated at times, and the capital may be seen negatively by the rest of the country. In Dublin, because so much of the development has been in the south of the city, there is a certain tension between those on either side of the river, north and south. The city as we know it is largely a product of the late 18th century and the 19th century. Apart from some churches and a few houses, nothing much antedates the 18th century. Other cities, I think, probably have more continuity, with their past in their architecture. Our city moved downstream by three-quarters of a mile out of its original confines, because the trading boats got bigger. It might have moved further but for the building of a railway bridge which blocked more development downstream. And, of course, the relationship between mountains and sea, both so close to Dublin, give it a particular character.

'The quality of life, I think, is better for most people but on the other hand two developments of the last 20 years are extremely

116

negative: the growth of unemployment – which is higher here than anywhere, except Spain, and the lack of social thought in connection with urban planning and domestic housing. But I think we are moving into a more favourable period. We are not going to solve unemployment and emigration until around 2010. By that time the number of young people coming on to the labour market will be just enough for the jobs available. I'd say that from then on you won't have significant emigration, but it will take another 20 years.

'The proportion of people who practise religion now has gone down but – apart from Poland – it is still probably the highest in Europe. But it is a mistake to think that the Church has had control over the State. It's had influence over the people, which 30 or 40 years ago operated directly through politicians, but apart from a very small number I don't recall, in my political lifetime, many politicians who have been distinctly operating on behalf of the Church. Now, politicians will have to be conscious of public opinion, and public opinion may be influenced by the Church on specific issues, and if the politicians challenge that opinion they may get the worst of it, as in the case of the divorce referendum. But the idea of the Church influencing the political structure simply isn't true. It has not been true for decades. We have to make up our own minds and we do so informed by the attitudes we have inherited, including the values derived from the churches to which we belong. But it's an independent view and not formed by anyone telling us what to do.

'Certainly the Church tries hard to influence people, especially at the moment on the two subjects of social justice and poverty. But I don't perceive it as having had much effect; in the area of divorce and contraception, there it clearly has influenced public opinion in the past and perhaps by concentrating too much on these matters it has lost the power to influence on other issues.

'But as I said I think we are moving into a much more favourable period. Regrettably a lot of our young, talented people are leaving and getting very good jobs abroad because the proportion of students completing secondary and tertiary education here is far higher than in Britain. While I recognise that some emigration is inevitable – I mean there is no way in which this country could achieve, as a European country, the scale of growth required to eliminate it completely – emigration is much higher than it need have been if we had handled our affairs better. But there are big movements back and forwards all the time. In the 1970s the numbers of people returning were greater than the numbers leaving. You see it all the time. In fact one of the things which increased the property prices rapidly in Dublin in 1989 was the small number of people who had done very well in England. They were returning, or contemplating a return, and they were all buying houses in the same area, adding just that much extra to the market and pushing up prices by 30 per cent in the South Dublin area.

'After 25 years in politics I don't want my life to be constrained by office again. Today I have more privacy, certainly, but also a freedom and opportunity to speak or write about things that interest me or that I wish to pursue. I never had any particular liking for public life for its own sake. Politics was a means of doing certain things when it seemed to me to be important. Obviously there were inhibitions about what could be said publicly at times. To some extent I have found the same in writing my autobiography. I'm not inclined to hit out at people but I think some people may be happier about the outcome than others. In an autobiography, however, I think you give something of yourself away not by what you say but by what you don't say. I'm interested to see what I learn about myself from the comments of those who read the book. They may tell me something I don't know at the moment.'

12

VOICES
The Whiskers

THIS IS A STORY of displacement, of turning the corner on home territory and suddenly discovering that you no longer belong. If anything it is the tale of a multiple identity crisis, a not uncommon fate for those who begin their days in the Six Counties of Northern Ireland. Like many, Charlie and Mariad Whisker started out with an equal distribution of unhelpful cultural baggage: he a Protestant, she a Catholic, each rooted in one or other camp of a perniciously futile social divide.

Charlie is a painter, a former art teacher who also works at the Windmill Lane recording studios in Dublin where he creates painterly effects as an overlay or canvas to rock videos. Mariad is a fashion designer with a studio and workshop off Grafton Street in Dublin, and an increasing reputation among the more original fashion cognoscenti. But, more than 20 years ago, before they had ever met, each had begun the quest for cultural equilibrium, impelled to leave Northern Ireland before the dreadful, crushing effect of unremitting violence demolished all individual and private hope. The mainland seemed the answer, but in England Charlie, who had been raised to think of himself as British, now found that the intense loyalties of that upbringing hadn't equipped him for London's more disengaged attitude to life.

Mariad, on the other hand, simply discovered that in England she was accepted as unmistakably Irish, and no fuss about North or South distinctions. 'In England,' she says, 'you can be Irish,

119

Scottish, English or Welsh and you are all regarded as equal. But here, in the Republic, I get the feeling that you can only be Irish.' In 1981, still seeking the ideal location, Charlie and Mariad – by now a couple – returned to Ireland, this time intending to establish a home in the South, and thus began the sharpest cultural shock of all, for suddenly neither seemed Irish, at least not in the Republic's terms.

'I just had some romantic idea of coming to live here,' says Charlie. 'I admit it wasn't very thought out but the notion was shattered within about half an hour of getting off the plane.' In the Republic they initially felt lost, neither Irish nor British. 'Just Northerners,' says Mariad, a euphemism for Outsiders which seemed to point up the shallowness of any 'united Ireland' aspirations in the South.

But ten years later Charlie and Mariad Whisker are still in the Republic, working in Dublin and living with their two children amid the leafy loveliness of a rolling garden surrounded by meadows, hedgerows and hills. That they have remained is perhaps an indication that Dublin's old, deep-rooted provincialism is slowly but finally disintegrating, breaking down under newer, exciting pressures imposed by a young population anxious now to find a room in the common European home.

'And the fact is that the physical beauty of Ireland has spoiled us,' says Charlie. 'We could never go back to living in London,' Mariad reflects, 'at least not unless we suddenly became mega-millionaires.' Just as it has enchanted so many before, Ireland has worked an ancient magic to beguile the Whiskers, despite their reservations. But, like all the world's uprooted people, they know, too, that wherever the wanderer disembarks may be a mistake in location. Charlie Whisker talked at length about his feelings: 'The various expressions of Irish culture were a well kept secret to me growing up – Irish language, music, the painters and writers etc. But maybe that is not so surprising as we were rich in our own culture in the North of Ireland. Socially I never really met or mixed with Catholic people until I was 17 when I went to art college. The opium den of the people. My parents were liberally minded from a Unionist, Protestant perspective and genuinely appalled by what came to light in terms of civil rights and the aftermath of violence. They were not members of any ''club'' and did not go to church, and were rather worried by my interests in a travelling band of evangelists –

"Henry's Revivals" – and in the groaning blues and gospel songs of America that I collected. My father gave me two bits of advice: "Always keep a few sheets of toilet paper in your wallet and stay out of churches." Sound advice really for a young man heading out into the complexity of life. Mind you, a handful of pink bumph dropping out of your Filofax, in Bewley's, is hardly *de rigueur*.

'Still, somewhere within me, lurking, is a rogue Protestant gene biding its time. That gene which is the cocktail mixed from your parents and your society and all that went before . . . is in us all. Intellectually I try to stifle it, keep it in chains, whisper, for fear of arousing it – but when it beats its drum forward I find myself at its mercy. Depending on the mix, the company, the few drinks and the argument I may well find myself waving the Union Jack proudly.

'As for any prejudice against Protestants down here – my general anti-social outlook allows me to push on past it. It's not so much against Protestants, but rather Northerners. I am happy living here and I've met so many genuinely good people. For the first three or four years I was dreadfully unhappy – the place to me was a great grey mess, too untidy, too casual. That was from 1981 when we arrived, in Cork, where I was teaching at art college. The Church and its travelling emissaries I saw everywhere – we couldn't rent a house, because we weren't married, so we lied. I watched priests leering and cheering as I protested against fox hunting and coursing. I saw five or six greyhounds stuffed into closed boots of cars, while hunters went to Mass. Roving priests, worse than any seller of encyclopaedias, had a large mucky brogue in our front door and – making themselves comfortable, after dislodging the cat – would pick into our pasts, wondering where "exactly" did we come from in Belfast. Now I'm content, they don't come around anymore and Ireland has become this pleasant peace, safe for my kids.

'In the North we are still confronted by the man with the gun who says, "I am right". I think once someone has been led to the point of pulling the trigger, they almost have to keep doing it. You have to believe in what you've just done or else you go insane. The social reality is that you are already insane.

'I came across a 16-year-old victim of assassination in Northern Ireland. It took half an hour for him to die in my arms. As his head came apart in my hands and his last breath gurgled blood I found my turning point in the North. Seeing a young life sacrificed, a lost

121

boy dying in my arms, in the dirt of a field, was such a soul-chilling event that the rest of my life and work are left in continual orbit of it.

'It was then that I decided to get out of Ulster. Like 95 per cent of the people there I was weary of it – now I was inspired by it. I thought that I had been through a unique experience, and personally I had – but it is not unique in Ireland – everyone has seen something or known someone that this has happened to. The tragedy you leave behind is the knowledge that there are 22-year-olds who have known nothing other than war.

'The emotional bedlam in me as a result of that death was so fantastical that I lost all control. I was laughing as I was crying, I had an anger I've never experienced before and a love that I never felt capable of. I had the deepest fears and yet unlimited courage, it seemed, all boiling frantically inside of me. I'd lost friends before to the violence of Northern Ireland, seen bombs tear the heart out of my home town – as everyone has up there – but I'd never seen such violence, so close, and I will never recover from it. Later I thought that maybe the only other experience that might come close to this extremity of emotion would be the birth of my first child. To see a life dawning as opposed to one fading. However, when that time came, at the very last moment, literally seconds – I was ushered out of the room by an uncaring fool of a doctor and I was denied it. I did see my second daughter, Domino, born and that was truly wonderful. This time I laughed while Mariad cried. There was some sense of a strange emotional reincarnation at that point – and for me it was very healing.

'My historical understanding was inadequate, the result of a biased history curriculum at school, a droning history master and a view of the girls' school next door, from the history room window. The glory of the British Empire shone very bright, casting a dark shadow over the story of Ireland. We were battery-raised Protestants, knowing little of the culture and language of the land we lived on. We were Protestants, and over there were the Catholics, and on it went. But I try to learn from it, to resensitise myself, to be more tolerant. We were taught intolerance – in a very keen, polished boy scout badge way we were taught intolerance – and could have passed, with flying colours, had it been a subject for O-level.

'My work as an artist is about me. I was part of the "me"

generation. I'm not driven by politics, landscape or portrait – only confused by them. It's my own past, present and future that concerns me – my ideas, romances, deviances, the loss of innocence etc. It works for me and it works for those who buy it. They're magical charms. Artists are a necessity, they are shamans, tolerated madmen, brokers in insanity. In tribal societies you see them dancing about, bedecked in skulls and beads – clowning-out fantasies. The artist is so tolerated and yet he may be a charlatan of some kind. Who knows what people are capable of?

'My experience of death is in every piece of work I do, sometimes blatantly – more often lurking in the background. I can't leave it out, it's part of my vocabulary as a painter, in fact it's part of my alphabet. Everything that I have painted since 1974 is an epitaph to that boy's death.

'At the moment I'm partly involved in a project – a musical based on the Irish Famine – this is very educational for me. It is a romance set against a background of famine so I've had to immerse myself in books and museums. The book, *The Great Hunger* was factually marvellous. The guy who has written the musical is very talented, Paddy Meegan, and I've learnt a lot from him on the subject of injustice. He is appalled by the violence of Ireland and the paramilitaries but he is staunchly Irish. I'm trying to come to terms with people who love their country – I personally don't have much feeling for my country, and I'm not even sure where it is. I wouldn't kill for Ireland, die for her or anything romantic like that. I'd just get on the boat. Northern Ireland is such a confused society, you're not sure where your loyalties lie. Nationalism is a curse, as much of a curse as organised religion is. It's a dangerous select club. It is that man with the gun who says, "I am right."

'Like Christianity and its Inquisition, the Conquistadors and Hiroshima – nationalism will only breed hatred and suspicion. Tolerant people who love their country are the only salvation. The idea of a musical about the Famine is very pertinent just now with the anniversary of the Irish Famine coming up, the awareness of famine throughout the world and the politics of hunger. Now, as then, we can feed people but choose not to. I think Shakespeare said something about . . . "where there is entertainment, there is learning . . ." I just hope that old history master goes along to this one, maybe he'll learn more in two hours on a soft seat than I did in six years on a hard school bench.

'But to go back to my original point, I feel disassociated from any kind of nationality. I live in Dublin, but don't feel a part of it. I don't really feel a part of Ireland. The bit that I know is a minefield of war and emotion. Politically Ireland, the South, is very dull. There is no one up there saying anything fresh, anything crucial. The very idea of watching televised Dail debates is as interesting to me as watching the Angelus. Politics is a real grey, grim world of suits, slapping or biting each other's backs. Let me hear someone who honestly wants to see divorce through, who admits to using a condom, who will ban the obscenity of blood sports, who will stand up to the burden of religious intolerance and religion itself.

'Anyway, our little family is safe here from snakes and poisonous insects, earthquakes and invasion. I like the complexity of a city life and the ease of a close countryside – so Dublin is ideal from that point of view, sufficiently cosmopolitan, buoyant and a lively mix of creatives. I find a strength of sincerity generally in the arts here, more so than elsewhere. In so many other cities, art is mere wall-paper – but there is an appreciation of it here and a creative integrity.

'Yet there is a contradiction here as well. Ireland has a great oral tradition in the South, always has had – but visually it is im-poverished. This is a personal view of course, but as an agricultural society it didn't develop visually. The country was to be used, worked in, milked, not tidied and preserved. Those quaint little thatched cottages, which are no more, were not built to look pretty, they were functional, just as those ugly white bungalows are today. And the awful bungalow blight from here to there and sideways doesn't matter a damn. I mean, there is a huge litter problem here. The bad side of Dublin is that it is an untidy dirty mess. From the shopper to the planner, it's ugly. It constantly amazes me – even friends of mine will think nothing of throwing an empty cigarette pack in the street, emptying their car ashtray in the Phoenix Park, or trashing a can of Coke over a hedge. I pick them up and give them back to people and they either don't know what you mean or get very defensive. There is no one telling anyone not to drop litter, no direction from the top. There is very little visual pride indigenous to this land or being imparted in education. As a lecturer in the college of art in Dublin part of my job was to assess applicants to the course. Out of a submission of maybe 600 portfolios we

124

would be required to pick 100 as successful worthy students. If we had been left to select on quality we would never have been able to choose more than 15 or 20 of them.

'Fortunately out of 100 or so we took aboard, many weak skilled students would aspire to greater things. Visual education at secondary level is in a dreadful state – I waded through seas of portfolios offering nothing more than a putrid flotsam of uninspired portraits of the Pope, JFK, John Lennon, pussycats and dogs, "my shoe", fruit, re-worked album covers of Horselips and Led Zeppelin. Can you believe students are still copying photographs of John F. Kennedy? Christ, they don't even know who he was. Awkward perspective ruled drawings of housing estates were being offered by kids from the Aran Islands, disintegrating shell craft and woolly gonks were stuffed in. Then maybe they'd been allowed to do an "abstract" – grotesque triangular shapes spewing forth like some demented Semtex-activated jigsaw.

'This all deviates from my point though – which is basically that I have none. I walked away from my point, slightly shell-shocked, caring little for politics and less for religion. I can't believe that people believe. It's an enigma to me. A difficult pancake! What do they believe? Why do they believe it? You're wandering along believing this thing and another believer comes up and shoots you in the head. You then have the misfortune to die in the arms of a non-believer. . .

'The Church here is too strong. There is nothing positive coming out. It's negative. It needs to learn some etiquette in this problem over North and South. It needs to embrace rather than confront with folded arms. For some reason I'm reminded of that bumper sticker – "If you love something, let it go. If it doesn't come back, hunt it down and kill it."

'I'm all for a second-coming, Krishna, Buddha, better not mention Mohammed – all the guys come on back and clear up the mess you started – or "was started on your behalf" is, I believe, how you word it. Magical lutes and blood to wine is fine by me. But from the ghosts of the Famine to the ghosts of Ulster where is the caring, embracing faith? Where is the shift to change and seeing the other point of view, to work with it and not agin it?

'I think that rogue Protestant gene is warming up again. Ireland is unique, though, partly to do with where it floats. Out there on the elbow of Europe, with nothing surrounding it, nothing passing through it on the way to some place else. Evolution rather than revolution. Though we somehow end up with both.

'I suppose my painting is often about disillusionment, that loss of innocence, a yearning for childhood. When you are young policemen are good, teachers are good, maybe even Charlie Haughey is good. They are good people – but as you become older and "wiser" you realise not all of them are good. At the heart of my own work is that loss of innocence, and the protected wonderful life of a child.'

Mariad also revealed her thoughts: 'To be quite honest I was horrified and disgusted at the reaction given to Austin Currie by some people down here when he stood during the Presidential election. All right he is a Northerner but he is a politician of proven integrity and commitment. Yet there were a few noisy people who thought he had no right to stand. I suppose I identified with him and his wife because the whole time I lived in England I always felt Irish. But when I came to live in Dublin I was made to feel that I was Northern. So here in my own country it is not my own country, it is not Northerners' own country. There is very definitely an attitude that we are Ulster people, and this is Ireland. It's not a question of the people of Southern Ireland being discriminatory – it's just my impression that they view Northern Ireland as a totally separate country. Charlie's background is completely different from mine. He is a Protestant from a Presbyterian background. He has always been British and I presume that in a strange way that gave him an identity crisis when he first went to England. But when he came back here it was even more acute. In England you can be Irish or Scottish, English or Welsh. Here you can only be Irish.

'But despite all my whingeing I do like it, I must say that. And I must say Dublin now is great, small enough still to be an intimate city but large enough to be cosmopolitan. It gets all the good films quickly and the theatre is strong. And the one aspect of it that I really love is that you can get a lovely house only half an hour from work. Huge garden and old trees, something very few of us could manage to possess in London. But I sometimes just wish Dublin was a bit more flexible and adventurous, you know? Mind you, it's my problem as well. It's up to me to decide if I'm not really making a living out of fashion and if I should be doing something else.

'I think if I was anywhere else than Dublin I would have done better professionally. The people who know fashion probably know me and would recognise what I have been doing, but that is not enough to make a living. I mean, I haven't really made a living out of my collections and for that reason I have to find a market elsewhere because the home demand here is not big enough to support what I do. I was talking to the designer, Michael Mortell, the other day and he had been reading in some magazine that Comme des Garçons had about 200 shops of their own in their native country, Japan. No wonder they have the money to achieve the kind of collections they do because they have an amazingly strong home base. I mean, there are certainly not 200 shops here that could sell my collection because of the price, so there is no way an Irish designer can make it in those terms in Ireland and then expand somewhere else. Also there is more support for designers in other countries, especially Italy, both from within and without the fashion industry. Fashion is respected in the business community whereas in Ireland I feel it is only tolerated. I mean, when you see pictures of Calvin Klein or Ralph Lauren at White House dinners or the like it's not because the First Lady thinks they're cute, it's because of what their business contributes to the economy.

'In Italy the textile manufacturers know that they have to depend on the designers to do something decent with the cloth they produce so it is in their interest to finance good designers. And then designers in turn influence the market so it's a sort of you-help-me-and-I'll-help-you arrangement. But I just find the exact opposite here. Because I'm small I pay through the nose for everything. I get credit on very little. I pay for all my fabrics pro forma [*upfront*] so in terms of making money it becomes a vicious circle. But I do now have a shop that sells me in New York, the Irish Secret, right down in SoHo near Spring Street. A friend from Canada said she had seen it when she was in New York so when I was there I called and loved it because it wasn't the typical stage Irish shop full of leprechauns and woolly jumpers. It sold good quality garments with the emphasis on fashion – not Irish for tweed's sake.

'My father started his working life as a panel-beater – beating the running-boards that they had on the side of old cars – so he's always worked with his hands. And then Mum always worked with clothing so I suppose my handiwork has come down directly through them. But none of my family now stays in Belfast. We were in a horrendous situation up there. Living in West Belfast, where my father carried out his business, wasn't particularly easy; living a middle class existence in an area that had, I believe, one of the highest levels of unemployment in Northern Ireland. At that time in the Seventies it was difficult to be a Catholic employer in an atmosphere of gross discrimination.

'The area we lived in was a huge overflow from the Falls Road. It seemed like they were demolishing the road from its source in the heart of Belfast city and leap-frogging the communities to the outer limits until the road almost ceased to exist and its inhabitants became totally displaced in a vast estate without decent amenities. Where we were situated in all this was a strategic nightmare – always seemingly caught in the middle of gun battles between the British Army and the IRA. Our next-door neighbours never seemed to have one intact pane of glass in their greenhouse with all the bullets they stopped. When friends, including Charlie, came to visit me from other slightly calmer areas of Belfast they usually spent their time lying between the wall and the settee when the gun battles started – much to my little sisters' amusement. The IRA would bury landmines in the road to try and blow up midnight army patrols and inevitably the only result would be all our windows blown in. In the end my father decided the only thing left to happen to us would be for one of the children to be hurt or killed, or even be seduced by the violence. This was a very real and terrifying possibility. Not long after I left Belfast to start college in England I read about the London car bombings in 1973 and was astonished to learn that girls I had gone to school with were arrested in connection with them.

'I couldn't believe that someone from the same cultural and social background as mine had reached a stage in their life where violence seemed the only viable expression of the social and political situation in the North. I realise that there must be a very fine line between words and action. I came from a Republican background in terms of the cultural aspects of Ireland – speaking Irish, learning about our history. But where does one cross over the line into terrorism? That Irish history thing is very powerful and ultimately, for some, totally seductive. It seems so easy for it to happen.

'But at the same time my dad's attitude was – "God, this is my home. We're not going to be driven out from our roots by Catholic, Protestant or British . . ." And I used to come home from Manchester and say: "You're one of the few people who are lucky enough to have the means to move. What are you doing living this

Seventy-five years after the Easter Rising, the GPO is still a focal point for dissent: Post Office workers protesting at the closure of rural post offices

Virgin's outlook on Aston Quay: the Virgin Megastore became central to the capital's great condom debate

A perpetual promenade along the East Pier of Dun Laoghaire

Well-crossed on O'Connell Street: a pilgrim loaded with religion

Dalkey fishing boats at Colliemore Harbour

Solidarity on Sean MacDermott Street

Bewley's, a magnet to Dublin's jeunesse dorée

The Mickey Dazzler outside the Gresham Hotel

*The hands-on presidency: Mary Robinson, President of the Irish Republic,
arriving to address the Irish Association for Victim Support*

Marsh's Library, one of the hidden gems of Dublin

Gandon's Custom House see through a Perspex awning at Tara Street Station

*A mixture of icons at the
Long Hall Bar on South
George Street*

The martello tower, now the James Joyce Museum, at Sandycove, its plump curve being repeated in the 'nautical house' designed by the distinguished Dublin architect Michael Scott

Open-plan paddock at Finglas

life?'' I remember wanting to surprise them one weekend by coming home unexpectedly from Manchester, and I got out of the taxi because no buses went up our road – they had all been burned – so you had to get a cab. I remember getting out and the driver had let me off right outside the house and I was walking up the driveway and halfway along I realised that the family weren't jumping up and down waving hello through the window, they were trying to tell me to get in quickly. I had just arrived in the middle of a huge gun battle and the bullets were flying up and down and I only just managed to get in when one came right through the front door and lodged in an inside wall. And then, one other time, I can't remember what happened but I think the house was broken into and it was a mess, and I don't know who was responsible that time but my Dad just said: "Right, that's it. I'm packing up." And within weeks the house was on the market and he and the family were down here. Today I would only go back to see Charlie's father who is still living up there but, other than that, I have no real inclination to return to Northern Ireland at all.'

OVER CENTURIES the mystic grandeur of Cathleen ni Houlihan has been the inspiration and the curse of Irish fashion, causing her to trail her cloaks and petticoats, her passionate beauty and defiant soul through the life and artistic sensibilities of a tiny nation. With poetry and plays Yeats, O'Casey and Synge ornamented her Mother Ireland symbolism. The actress Siobhan McKenna endowed the legends with a keening resonance that moved audiences to tears. But, somewhere along the road, the brave Cathleen became bowdlerised by tourism, turning up as the noble ghost at every packaged 'medieval' banquet, or as the clichéd finale to every dollar-conscious fashion show.

Through the Fifties only one designer in Dublin broke free of Celti-land to rise to international status. Sybil Connolly's skill as a couturier proved that one could creatively exploit native tweeds and linens and exquisite lace to achieve something far beyond the hackneyed romanticism that Irish fashion had become. Connolly's substantial reputation abroad inspired others in the Sixties and Seventies to aspire to similar prestige. Some, like Ib Jorgensen, were well established emigrés in Ireland, sophisticates who enjoyed their somewhat pioneering role in reversing the country's customary one-way traffic out of Irish ports. Irene Gilbert and Clodagh, however, were indigenous designers who, like Connolly, understood the intricacies involved in re-interpreting traditional characteristics for far-flung appeal.

Even so these were names creating bespoke, formal fashion for a privileged clientele. At this time Irish dressing was still very firmly rooted in the draught-excluding merits of mohair capes and matching tammies, and all those tweeds made for longevity. Nevertheless no one could confuse Dublin's Grafton Street for Princes Street in Edinburgh. The cut of the clothes in both capitals might have been conventional, but while Princes Street was sedate in colour Grafton Street's palette packed an exhilarating punch.

Over subsequent years Irish designers have retained this exuberance, enlivening the universal mood for black with stunningly coloured wraps, or threading otherwise sombre tweeds with little pimples of berry red, holly green and glowing broom yellow. And, while Common Marketry has given young Ireland a new European coat to wear, opening the doors of shops to some of the most influential of Continental designs, so it has also encouraged a generation of young, keenly competitive fashion creators who know that in a small country of just over three million people home demand is not enough. To sustain excellence and financial viability, talent must be pitched at wider horizons and be sure enough of itself to stand exposure in some of the most critical markets in the world.

But like Scotland, Ireland is still hindered in establishing a generally recognised fashion identity by its lack of an internationally distinguished fashion school which can stretch latent talent towards goals of excellence and encourage all the necessary intellectual and business disciplines. Of the currently impressive posse of designers in Dublin Paul Costelloe, the most established, studied in New York which may account for his casual but infinitely stylish approach to dressing. Michael Mortell, without doubt the most notable son of fashion that Mallow in County Cork has produced, learned his craft at Manchester Polytechnic, then St Martin's in London. John Rocha, half Chinese, half Portuguese and born in Hong Kong, is a graduate of Croydon Art College, and Mariad Whisker, a native of Belfast, whose clothes evoke some of the asymmetrical fluency of Yohji Yamamoto, studied at Manchester Art College.

To this small band of distinction Lainey Keogh's knitting talent is added, lifting cropped tops, boleros and jackets out of the prosaic and on to a level where they appear as commanding style statements in themselves. Essentially Keogh's gift is to combine stitches ancient and modern (custom-honoured Celtic cables, honeycombs and bobbles mixed with sharper architectural outlines). As a result the texture of each hand-knitted and crocheted garment is fascinatingly different although the overall shape stays true to each season's silhouette.

Lainey, in her mid-thirties, first gained recognition a couple of years ago when her work was chosen by the Paris couturier, Christian Lacroix, for one of the major textiles awards in France, the Prix de Coeur. Since then her designs have expanded, reflecting decorative influences from numerous cultures, but they still retain a distinctive Irishness in use of colour : fuchsia and hedgerow green, russet and inky mountain blues lit with shafts of rock pinks and dazzling yellow. In fact Lainey Keogh is a good example of how the gifted can sometimes beat the system for she has never had any formal fashion training. After studying medical technology she worked in the pathology department of a Dublin hospital and it was there – on becoming inundated with knitting orders as a result of wearing one of her own jumpers – that she decided to test the commercial potential and quality of her skill by changing full time to fashion.

In contrast Quin and Donnelly's knitting is svelte rather than craft-based. It possesses a certain Parisian *élan* with long narrow skirts and leggings in the finest rib, and cultivated, baggy jackets defined by interesting lapels. Clever knits that can carry women stylishly through the sleekest cities in the world.

Louise Kennedy's clothes are reaching the same destinations, principally on the back of her most famous customer, Mary Robinson, President of the Irish Republic. A graduate of Dublin's Market and Design College, and the Grafton Academy, Louise created the President's much acclaimed inaugural outfit, a short *soigné* coat of deep violet wool over a long, curvaceous jacket in amethyst moiré silk. Like many female designers Louise knows the value, in comfort and self-confidence, of good working clothes for career women, and places great emphasis on memorable cuts for jackets which then become the focus for an outfit's entire look. Anticipating the melting European trade barriers after 1992, she is among those Dublin designers now securing important contracts with Britain and the Continent.

But however creative and original an Irish designer might be there is one inescapable problem: the difficulty in obtaining significant financial backing on starting out. 'If you are a young, unknown talent,' says Mariad Whisker, 'then you have the greatest difficulty in gaining any help from the various state bodies which can offer incentives. In my experience they always play safe and go for the conventional or established names. And to some extent I also think that's true of the Dublin clientele. This city is not yet really self-assured enough to go big on the innovative as other capital cities do. But, because of the size of the population, there is a very small market here, anyway, for designer clothes.'

Sometimes, of course, there are certain fashion snobberies at work among the public: a certain sniffy suspicion that in matters of style the only good things are those that come from abroad and carry a potent label. But anyone who buys fashion first and foremost to flaunt an international name has no real understanding of the art of dressing – a fact conceded by many of the great designers themselves. In fact, such insistence on the big names does nothing but mark out the provincial, over-dazzled by others' fame.

'Except among the young kids who put their own look together, there isn't much individualism among Dubliners who can afford to pay high prices for their clothes,' says Mariad. 'And at the moment among many of those I know there is this almost anti-fashion thing of wearing a big sloppy sweater, leggings and a long skirt. Very much the hippy fashion of the Sixties, and all right as far as it goes but it doesn't say a thing about individuality. In fact it says the opposite because there is so much of it around. To me the hippy thing, maybe because I remember it first time round, was originally very exciting, but now . . . well, it's like wearing a 1940s suit twenty years later. So soon afterwards it simply doesn't make a style statement. You've got to wait until it's completely out of memory, and then when it has become such a brand new thing again you can do your own thing with it.'

John Rocha's story is proof that fashion is as merciless for the acclaimed as for the beginner. His problems, in the late Eighties, sprang from his very success as an arbiter of ethereal *chic*: long, floaty dresses in pale, delicate linens beneath tail-coats and panelled jackets of masterly cut and flair. But demand from both home and overseas was far exceeding John's ability to deliver. His very gift was driving him into the classic rag-trade trap and to solve the nightmare he had to close his Chinatown shop in Dublin. Then with his wife and children, he went off to Milan to work as a designer with Refraction, returning to Ireland every few months to supervise the Chinatown line which was still in production.

The Rochas stayed in Italy for a year, then A-Wear came calling. This young, vibrant department store in Dublin is part of the Brown Thomas group and now provides the backing for the Chinatown label, 60 per cent of which goes abroad. 'My best foreign customers are Italy, France and the United States. On reflection I would say that my year in Italy was of vital importance because it brought maturity. I learned first hand how the Italians organise their business, the importance of infrastructure and of being able to control the detail. To be a success this business has to be like a table with four legs. One for finance, one for manufacture, one for design and the fourth for distribution. If any leg is missing then all of them are in trouble.'

John's wife, Odette, is involved in styling and marketing the collection which now draws on 15 Irish factories for the manufacture. Prices remain some of the keenest for designer clothes and business has tripled in the past three years. 'I enjoy making clothes that look good on people,' he says. 'I get a kick out of it, but the hype of fashion doesn't turn me on at all. If I'd been skilled enough I'd have rather been a professional footballer than a designer.'

Similarly Michael Mortell, festooned with all the design prizes that Ireland can offer, would rather have been an artist. 'I did the compulsory hippy thing in London in 1968 but back in Mallow my elder sister kept telling me that there was no money in painting. Dress designing was the thing, she said. She told me that in Manchester there was this scholarship going to study fashion, and just to get her off my back I applied.' Mortell insists that fate, rather than talent, decreed he won, and now, reflecting on his undoubted stature in the trade, he says simply : ' Well, I seem to be handy at it, but I'm not an undiscovered Yves Saint Laurent, or anyone like that.'

Like Rocha, he regards Armani, Miyake, Gaultier, Yohji Yamamoto and Montana as the style mentors of the age. 'But living in Ireland,' he says, 'you are very isolated from the rest of the fashion world, and maybe that makes you too in awe of the big names. But when the spending euphoria of the Eighties was over

I decided to re-think my whole concept about being a designer in Ireland. With the recession I had to rationalise everything and so I stopped asking myself: how would Bloomingdale's in New York like this? Instead I had to be disciplined and consider only how a line would go down with the market here. Sure, I'd like to be Yohji or Montana, but if after ten years I'm not, then there is no point in moaning.

'A designer has to examine the best of what he does and concentrate on that. I rationalised my business by cutting out diversification for a few seasons and I just focused on distinctive rainwear, always in demand here because of the climate.' What Mortell is saying, in fact, is that the days of artistic self-indulgence are over for fashion designers. Meeting delivery dates is the urgent priority now. 'That doesn't mean a collection has to be boring because of lack of detail. In fact, achieving an interesting shape, with no distractions on the surface, is a greater challenge. But there were times when I'd hold a whole collection up in order to experiment with a pocket. Now, it's perhaps a sign of maturity or survival that I believe a pocket is a pocket.'

At the start of every season, reflects Mortell, a designer must be in with that first rush of business, and that requires getting quality-controlled garments to the retailers precisely on time. But one of the difficulties for Dublin designers is that the Republic doesn't possess a comprehensive textile industry. Unless they are working exclusively in tweed or linen (produced in the North), designers must rely on foreign suppliers for everything from outer fabrics through to linings, buttons and even zips. This obviously pushes up production costs but it is also precarious in that Irish designers rarely need to order in great bulk – again because of the small home market – and this can mean that when the heat is on with the big international companies Dublin's demands fall to the end of the queue, thus jeopardising agreed deadlines with the stores. As with Paul Costelloe, Mortell steers clear of a structured, frocky look, preferring a willowy line which fits into a busy woman's wardrobe without complications.

Costelloe, particularly, knows how to exploit the American formula for supremely easy yet elegant separates, but in the process he gives them an Irish twist. 'I enjoy designing dresses now and then,' he says. 'But separates allow for much more variety. I like the look of fabric on fabric, colour on colour . . . yet still following the same theme. The effect is interesting, and that for me is better than a straight, unbroken line.'

A tall, lean, sandy-haired Celt who looks more like a sports-loving farmer than a garment-maker to the modish, including Britain's younger royals, Costelloe, too, has little time for the raucous self-regard which often surrounds the fashion world. Instead he is a man very aware of his trade's pressing realities: 'Behind me I have a factory with a lot of workers and all of us know only too well that this can be a hell of a business. The vital thing is not to be distracted from what you do best by the whims of other designers.'

Twenty years ago most people still regarded Irish fashion as a rudimentary wardrobe of items like a Donegal tweed coat, Aran sweater and perhaps a collar in Carrickmacross lace. But in the widest context it wasn't until Armani and Kenzo came along that the world realised that tweed could be used in exciting and un-expected ways. The best of Dublin's current designers have embraced that challenge, free of any inhibitions about using the cloth in only the inherited manner. Many of them work directly with Ireland's specialist textile mills, gaining from the liaison that these plants themselves have established with leading international designers like Dior, Saint Laurent, Armani, Ralph Lauren and Donna Karan.

Even so there is an winsome Irishness about the best of Dublin fashion. It is difficult to define exactly but maybe it has something to do with the sporty relish of so much Irish life: the races, the summer festivals up and down the country. That certain open-air swagger you find in Ireland, uniting the toffs in their Georgian houses with the Joycean traipsers dressed up to the Force Nines on Dun Laoghaire pier.

13

THEMES
Drink

THREE YEARS AGO the unimaginable occurred when 3,000 barmen in Dublin and its vicinity threatened to strike over a proposal to extend opening hours which would allow the pub door to swing free until midnight on weekdays through the summer. In return for the extra hours involved the bar staffs' union was insisting on an increase of IR £31.07 a week, plus an added day off every fortnight. Predictably the Licensed Vintners Association shrugged off the claim as absurdly unrealistic. Meanwhile in the backroom of the Palace Bar the patois was more vigorous: 'Isn't it the divil that a man finds a bunch of Bolsheviks standing between himself and his pint? Aren't the lads only being asked to work 24 more hours a year? And for them to base any part of their negotiation on the abolition of the Holy Hour is a matter of grave reprobation. Sure the buckos are being paid for that already.'

For a while the clientele attacked its stout with the intensity of a condemned man setting about his final breakfast. Then when time was called at the very last eleventh hour 'an amicable compromise' was announced. The barmen accepted a more moderate increase to their wallets and it was agreed that on winter weekdays pubs would open at 10.30 a.m. and close at 11 p.m. In summer they would remain open till 11.30 p.m., and throughout Dublin (the only place in Ireland where it existed), the Holy Hour would be abolished.

That 60 minutes of non-sacramental grace, alternatively known as the HH, was when bars closed during the afternoon. Of course,

137

in the more idiosyncratic drinking shops it was often little more than make-believe with favoured customers, like the literary coterie of Patrick Kavanagh, Brian O'Nolan (alias Flann O'Brien and Myles na Gopaleen) and Brendan Behan, being allowed to sink deeper into the mahogany snugs as if they were confessionals.

But it has always been a characteristic of Dublin's large floating bar trade that the solitary drinker is as vital to the general chat as any bunch of bookish exhibitionists firing loquacious broadsides into the fug. In his book *No Laughing Matter, The Life and Times of Flann O'Brien*, the writer Anthony Cronin recalls that O'Brien's own definition of a good bar was: 'Quiet and comfortable, softly lighted and a boon to any sensible, tired person who wants his stimulant without being jostled and who does not concern himself with social trends or think that a well-dressed woman in a pub is an outrage that imparts a sourness to the drink.' Drinking for O'Brien, as Cronin observes, was a serious almost sober business, but then it is in the nature of the Dublin bar-fly to turn a cliché on its head. According to the distinguished international journalist Peter Lennon, the trick is: 'Partly a way of displaying your Dublin credentials, sending reassuring signals that you are of the same tribe – relaxed about drink; mocking, at least privately, of religious beliefs, and privy to all mortifications of a puritanical society dying to be pagan.'

The bar-fly, then, is the Dubliner incarnate, an individual whose relish of language suggests a life of brilliance but whose everyday existence may be nailed down to a scene of small eventualities. 'To be honest with you,' this bar-fly will confide in whispered intimacy, 'there isn't a politician in the whole of Ireland who would make a body feel confident about being here. I'll tell you the truth of it, the state of the country can be condensed into two words: bloody ridiculous. There's not a hint of a job for the likes of those without one while all the politicians do is push up the price of a pint thus further ruining the social fabric of the country . . .'

Flann O'Brien called bars 'licensed tabernacles' and certainly it is true that the pub in Ireland is as rooted in the national character as the church. In Dublin, around Trinity College and Baggot Street particularly, it prides itself on being the pillar of the intelligentsia. In the wild isolation of the West, the barman is the most informed individual in the parish, the shrewdest tradesman too, selling not just liquor and Orangina but anything from firelighters to tombstones. 'You might say that the barmen in this country are the best in the world, and I'd agree with you,' says the bar-fly. 'In Dublin they pull a pint of Guinness as if they were pouring poetry into a glass and that sort of respect is sadly lacking right through society now. I'll grant you that the barmen have been good to old Dublin but – if I may paraphrase Brendan Behan – hasn't old Dublin been good to the barmen as well?'

Within the sanctuary of the pub the Dublin tendency to take everything said as personal is accompanied by the art of circular argument which may keep a conversation between strangers going for hours.

'Isn't this one pound coin terrible tinny money altogether?' says one drinker to another. 'It's a national disgrace and very confusing for the old people. The Government shouldn't have introduced any of those new coins until all the old people were dead.' There is no logic to the argument, yet it has its point. The travel writer Jan Morris believes you need only stand in the door of a Dublin bar and shout above the general hum: 'Do you think he should have gone over?' and back will come a chorus of two replies: 'Ah, not without telling the wife'; or 'And why shouldn't he? Didn't his father do the same?'

The reluctance to accept any conclusion to anything except one's own laps over into attitudes to punctuality. The Progressive Democrat politician, Mary Harney, maintains that an appointment in Ireland – even in Government circles – is 'a matter of approximate time and never intended as on the dot'. This leisurely rhythm must also in some way account for the emotional blackmail and ingenuity which Dublin barmen apply when calling time: 'Lads, lads, come on now, will you let this poor fella behind the counter get to a dance.' That cry, regularly heard from beneath the gantry on a Friday night, is matched by the solicitous coaching going on around the tables: 'There's good lads, now, if you just stand up at least you'd make me think you might be going.'

Of course, in the old days a barman could always rely on his customers in time of trouble. The assailant's 'hand over the money, or I'll twist your head off' would, they say, be met with a rapid scuffle as the clientele closed in around the offender, accompanying its actions with a thrust of broken chair legs to the malevolent wretch's ribs. Those days are gone. Pub crime now operates on no such amateurism. Today it mimics terrorism or the sudden, inexplicable violence of New York. One more unimaginable thing: in some parts, the Dublin barman is demanding danger money.

14

CITY, STATE AND CHURCH
The Great Magnifico

FLORENTINE MAGNIFICO, street fighter, nationalist rabble-rouser, glad-handing dictator, mafioso don . . . for almost three decades Charles James Haughey, the demon king of Irish politics, has strutted around the country, trailing this gaudy litany behind him. Yet the real personality of the man remains elusive.

Dublin's attitude towards Taoiseach Haughey has always been complex: craven loyalty on the part of his acolytes has its roots in a sentiment once effectively voiced by Ray MacSharry, then deputy leader of Fianna Fail and later the EC Agricultural Commissioner. Just a few hours before an abortive coup to oust the party supremo, MacSharry warned the movement: 'Anyone who votes against Charles Haughey will never be forgiven.' But among the electorate admiration both for Haughey's riches and for the brazen quality of his grip on power is tempered by mistrust. After nearly 30 years he is now among the curios of the political world: a leader whose repeated fallibility has scarcely diminished the potency of his name.

Ever since 1970, when he was implicated in a bizarre arms smuggling trial but survived the scandal relatively intact, Charles Haughey has been surrounded by gales of controversy, his reputation with the public swinging madly from that of manipulative buccaneer to Irish Thatcherite. Although pursued largely on his own behalf, his considerable entrepreneurial skills have brought him a certain respect. He is, after all, a multi-millionaire in a tiny country, his fortune deriving originally from property deals. On the whole the Irish are not stuffy or snobbish about how a man comes by his money but for all those who claim that the extent of Haughey's fortune is a commendable distinction there are others who argue cogently that Ireland's smallness should be its very reason for shunning the huge disparity between the wealthy and the poor.

The magnifico tag, one suspects, pleases him most of all for it confirms his upward climb from humble beginnings in the pinched, claustrophobic streets of Marino in North Dublin. Today he still lives in North Dublin but Marino has been exchanged for Kinsealy and the squat, red-brick of the working class has given way to a Georgian mansion sitting in 200 acres of parkland, with hunters in the paddock. In town Haughey delights in good restaurants, extravagant company and the attentions of handsome women. Yet on holiday he reverts to his country-squire persona, spending most of his time at Inishvickalaun, the island he owns at the mouth of Dingle Bay in Kerry.

There his demands for privacy are now part of the region's folklore. One story insists that Haughey imported German stone-masons to build his island home because he didn't want the locals to know his business. Certainly it is true that he has always been a secretive man, and one who seeks insulation by employing the kind of party henchmen who are adept at intrigue and the heavy elbow. And it may be that his enigmatic nature has been his surest asset, for throughout his career Haughey has dodged political death repeatedly, leaping through hoops of fire like a circus veteran whose flamboyant risks mask an inscrutable soul. In O'Connell Street Charles Haughey, during a General Election campaign, goes walkabout with the rest of them, pressing the flesh of bemused commuters more intent on squashing into rush-hour buses than applauding the politicians' quick round of glad-handing. He dashes into a leading unisex hairdresser's in the hope of catching the votes of the blow-dried electorate. Later, studiously avoiding a Chinese restaurant next door and an old man on a bike who addresses him as 'Ireland's Al Capone', the Taoiseach pats a few young dissident heads on the pavement. 'That,' says one mother to her infant school son, 'is the fella who's meant to be governing the country.' Politicians learn to exit on such lines which is probably why Haughey often greets voters with the engine of his official limousine still running.

In 1990 Haughey's mythic powers of recovery were demonstrated during the Presidential election, when it was alleged that in 1982 his political colleague and old pal Brian Lenihan had attempted to persuade the then President, Dr Patrick Hillery, to make Haughey an unelected Taoiseach because of the grave crisis facing the Government of Fine Gael. Brian Lenihan denied the allegations and Fianna Fail exploded in unconvincing moral outrage, accusing all opposition parties of stooping to dirty tricks. Such histrionics, however, did nothing to save Lenihan, himself a Presidential contender. Haughey, having publicly professed his confidence and faith in Lenihan, within hours then sacked him as Tanaiste (deputy Prime Minister) and Defence Minister in order to placate the Progressive Democrats, the minority partners in the coalition. The ultimate crony had become the ultimate victim, not much of a thank-you gift to a trusting friend.

The scandal brought with it not so much Dublin's customary relish of dignitaries caught in a verbal brawl but one more salutary indication of the non-accountability of those in political office. Despite its protestations of innocence Fianna Fail was perceived to have attempted to meddle with the neutrality of the Presidency. And just as it presumed a divine right to rule in Ireland, so it also presumed the appointment of President to be in its gift. This, in fact, was the second time in 16 months that the bold Charlie had inadvertently led the people to question the quality and integrity of those chosen to conduct their affairs.

Like many dictators Taoiseach Haughey, the Republican who would be king, has only one real objective: to rid himself of opponents, gain total control and keep it. To this end he has so obsessively stifled dissent within his party (which he has led since 1979) that while it rates high in exploiting the main chance, Fianna Fail lacks philosophical debate and possesses no coherent plan of what it represents. Those front-bench spokesmen reckless enough to waver from the Haughey line are publicly humiliated by their master. P. J. Mara, the Taoiseach's confidant and press secretary of the party, once remarked that all Fianna Fail utterances should reflect: *'Uno duce, una voce'*. It was the closest Haughey had come to snatching at the mantle of the Pope, and in the pubs of Dublin that night the wags were noting Ireland's increasingly European persuasion now that 'Charlie's buckos are calling the shots in Italian.'

Despite his brilliant opportunism – the nippy shifts from republican and Catholic fundamentalism when in opposition; the stance of conciliatory European during Ireland's Presidency of the EC – the recurring flaw in Charles Haughey's make-up has been a curious lack of vision; a failure to realise that the old wheeler-dealer network with which Fianna Fail has served the country for so long now possesses little relevance to the social issues and sophisticated aspirations of a new and exceptionally well educated electorate.

At his own Christian Brothers school in Fairview, Dublin, Haughey was noted for an academic excellence sharpened by street cunning. The hunger to succeed not only gained him numerous scholarships but also led to sports distinctions in hurling and Gaelic football, and always driving his ambition to be a winner was the desire to make big money. For this reason he chose accountancy, rather than, say, medicine, joining Fianna Fail and quickly mixing with the influential. His adroit business skills became apparent very early, and in 1951 Haughey gilded his future by marrying the daughter of the man who would succeed Eamon de Valera, the late Sean Lemass, one of the most enlightened of Ireland's modern politicians.

The prospects seemed golden then, and by the mid-Sixties he was not only flying high in the Government of Honest Jack Lynch but assiduously traversing the country, cultivating allegiances in some of the most remote but crucial western tracts and assuring 'the plain people of Ireland' that they were the keystone to his political success. 'He looked people in the eye, spoke well and listened attentively,' recalled *Irish Times* political journalist Denis Coghlan. 'And the men from Binghamstown, Emlybeg and Bangor knew him as one of their own.' Well equipped with grassroots savvy, his career found real dynamism between 1966 and 1970 when as Minister of Finance he was responsible for a whole raft of benign measures aimed at assisting the weakest in society. Free transport, telephones and TV licences were given to pensioners, and Haughey, who has always liked to consider himself something of a Medici, also enabled artists to live in Ireland with income-tax exemption.

It was during these years that the gulag genre of speculative building triumphed in Dublin over the Georgian conservationist campaigns. Haughey was among those who made serious money out of the boom which inflicted a heavy price on the harmonious architecture of the city. Yet, if anything, having pots of money increased Haughey's popularity at this time. He might indeed have been considered 'a bit of a chancer' but at least people hoped that here was a man who would manage the country's wallet as well as he obviously did his own.

Then everything appeared to disintegrate with the eruption of savage tribalism in the North. In January 1967 the Northern Ireland Civil Rights Association was founded to campaign for justice and equality of opportunity for the Catholic population. By the end of 1968 its peaceful demonstrations were already being confronted by violence waged by the Protestant armed police battalion, the B-Specials, and Loyalist extremists, but it was in 1969 that the full horror of the blood-letting was really apparent. In January the People's Democracy march from Belfast to Derry was attacked at Burntollet Bridge and by August the Bogside in Derry and the Falls Road in Belfast were under siege which led to the British troops being called in to maintain order.

Like everyone, Charles Haughey was appalled at what he saw but complicating his republicanism were the blazing emotions contained in his family history. Both his parents were from County Derry and his relatives' experience of the prejudice and oppression, which for generations had poisoned so much of life in the North, very clearly affected his own political psyche and judgment. On 6 May, he, along with the Donegal politician, Neil Blaney, was dismissed from the Government by Jack Lynch and 22 days later both men were arrested for conspiracy to import arms which were allegedy destined for Catholics across the border. By July Blaney, a gruff, uncompromising but shrewd politician, had been discharged but Haughey was forced to defend himself in court and although he was acquitted on 23 October the whiff of gunsmoke clung to him for years, consigning him to political limbo.

But the old craftiness hadn't deserted Charlie Haughey. Instead of languishing he once again stomped the country, from Donegal to Kerry, holding meetings in cold, miserable halls and ingratiating himself with narrow, forsaken communities by exploiting the primitive strength of politics played for patronage and favour.

In the end, of course, Haughey's commitment to lacklustre constituencies helped to swing fortune in his direction at the Dail. In the 1977 election Jack Lynch had been returned with an historic majority but the new politicians included many of Charlie's compadres from those far-flung seats. When the leadership battle arose two years later Lynch's preferred heir, George Colley, found himself pushed out of the premiership (although he had virtually full Cabinet support) by a 'peasants' revolt' on the back benches. So Haughey assumed power and although the opportunity was there then to turn Fianna Fail into a modern, social democratic movement but one which would still represent its peculiar traditional mix of business, rural and working-class allegiances, the Taoiseach chose to make it an intensely centralised party where any dissent is branded as betrayal and paranoia seems to be a required attribute of Cabinet office.

This obsession with loyalty is not surprising, perhaps, since Haughey's initial Cabinet was mostly composed of members who had been vehemently opposed to him. But it sprang principally from Colley's public refusal to pledge fealty to the man who had robbed him of the top prize in 1979. In ensuing years this atmosphere of suspicion led Haughey's fanatical supporters into aberrant behaviour. The phones of two prominent political journalists were tapped; one Minister secretly taped another's conversation, then had the tape transcribed at Garda headquarters in Dublin, and in one of two general elections in 1982 Haughey's own political agent, Padraig O'Connor, was reported to be under police investigation for voting not only in his chief's home ground of Kinsealy but also in neighbouring Malahide. A man who, in the words of Conor Cruise O'Brien, one of Charles Haughey's most implacable enemies, loved democracy not wisely but too well.

Irish politics has never lacked either passionate intensity or elements of farce but over his years in power (and Haughey had by now achieved his fourth term) the exposure of Fianna Fail's cabals, its intrigues, double-speak and the baying and brawling at Leinster House – the seat of government itself – led to sustained criticism and anger in the press. 'The undead Taoiseach' is Cruise O'Brien's Gothic phrase for Charles Haughey, and the *Sunday Tribune* used equally vigorous prose in urging an end to political chicanery. In 1982 it wrote: 'It is . . . helping to spread the conviction among ordinary people that many of those who present themselves on political platforms are fortune-hunters and shysters . . .'

For his part Haughey has been unequivocal in his condemnation of the press. There is a story told in the Palace Bar that when he once dismissed an *Irish Times* reporter with the words, 'The press hates me and I hate the press,' he then demanded to know who was responsible for writing the newspaper's editorials. When the hapless reporter disclaimed personal responsibility, Haughey snapped: 'They read as if they have been done by an old woman sitting in a bath with the water getting cold around her fanny.'

When he became Taoiseach in 1979 Haughey made Northern Ireland his priority amd with considerable skill he managed to persuade a reluctant Mrs Thatcher that a radical new British initiative was urgently required. On their first meeting in London he applied the old Haughey charm, flattering her with the gift of an antique silver teapot and reminding the British Prime Minister that political leaders acquired a place in history not by beating inflation but by solving great conflicts. Suddenly it appeared that Mrs Thatcher had found an Irish politician with whom to do business. In December 1980 she flew to Dublin with Lord Carrington and Geoffrey Howe to sign a joint communiqué which recognised the need to consider the totality of relationships between Britain and Ireland. Something momentous had occurred, placing the problem of Northern Ireland in a refreshingly new inter-governmental context, but here again Haughey's lack of vision tripped him up. While Mrs Thatcher dealt with the Unionists' predictable fury, reticence was what was needed on the part of Dublin. But Dublin in the form of Government Minister Brian Lenihan made the diplomatic gaffe of overselling the talks and this so infuriated Mrs Thatcher she retreated from any mould-breaking proposals.

From then on mutual estrangement set in, deepening first with Britain's handling of the H-Block hunger strikes at the Maze Prison in Belfast, and later with the Falklands War. Ironically it was Haughey's old rival, the Fine Gael leader Garret FitzGerald, who eventually gained the benefits of that extravagant notion of a place in history when, after patient and gentlemanly coaxing, he gained Mrs Thatcher's signature on the Ango-Irish Agreement during his time as Taoiseach in 1985.

Profligate spending and wild foreign borrowing marked Charles Haughey's second period in office in 1982. At the time he was attempting to retain the improbable support of fractious independent deputies who included one Dublin maverick socialist and three Marxists. Over the numerous crises and internal attempts to axe him from the Fianna Fail leadership, Haughey's fanatics have remained true, but it has been their republican intransigence on the North and such issues as contraception, abortion and divorce which has often made him the prisoner of atavistic thinking. This, as much as his dictatorial manner, has forced out some of the most able men and women in the party – Desmond O'Malley and Mary Harney who in 1985 formed the Progressive Democrats and were followed by Bobby Molloy and Pearse Wyse.

Launched on an overdraft of £5000, the PDs see their constituency as mainly coming from Dublin's disaffected young. The problem there, of course, is that many of Dublin's disaffected young fell off the electoral register because lack of jobs has forced them to emigrate. Even so, in 1989 the PDs found themselves in the frailest of coalitions with Fianna Fail, no one appreciating the piquancy of this closeness more than Dessie O'Malley, the Minister of Industry and Commerce. Bad blood had been boiling between him and Haughey ever since the gun-running fiasco. In the early 1980s it reached an intolerable temperature for O'Malley when, on the issue of public credibility and performance, he challenged Haughey's leadership. But, like so many other attempts, this one dwindled into abysmal failure as Ray MacSharry issued his infamous warning.

By March 1987 FitzGerald's own coalition Government was sliding into a slump of depressing economic statistics and party infighting restrained by Fianna Fail standards but still damaging. So, despite its latent mistrust of Haughey, the country turned to him again and he, at last anxious to redeem his past record as a Taoiseach who delivers nothing but empty financial promises, confounded his critics by becoming more Thatcherite than Thatcher, demanding the most drastic cuts in public spending for 25 years. And it worked. By early 1989 his fiscal policies were proving successful in restoring vitality to a dilapidated economy. Statesmanship rather than flagrant self-preservation appeared to be ruling his thoughts on the North, and in general an air of consensus government seemed to be endowing Irish politics with a mantle of realism and maturity, though it also reflected the public's irritated exhaustion with a glut of general elections. More than any other Western country Ireland was culturally and emotionally in transit between old dreams and new, a journey which always requires deft and courageous bridge-work on the part of politicians. But here was Haughey finally reflecting his young country's desire to be rid of stultifying provincialism and sly, backwoods fixing. And then he threw it all away.

In the hope of gaining an overwhelming majority, he called another unwanted general election in 1989 and when the results were seen to be inconclusive he then refused to concede an inability to govern without the aid of a coalition. The cloak of statesmanship proved threadbare, nothing more than a temporary protector of a minority administration. For their part the Progressive Democrats, Fine Gael and Labour were adamant that Haughey would be in breach of the Constitution if he attempted to govern by absolute rule. But after a month of impasse and crisis-management the wheel turned full circle for the Taoiseach who during his years in the Dail has achieved so many about-turns on policy and principle that, by popular definition, he is known as 'Kentucky-fried Charlie, the leader on a spit'. In the end, by horse-trading of unprecedented finesse, he managed to cobble together the most improbable Government the country had ever seen.

But of all those he approached it is O'Malley who most influences his fate. Yet once again the old battered survival kit appears to be doing the business. The questionable nationalist rhetoric and Tammany Hall glad-handing have been cast aside as Haughey sets his cap at statesmanship once more. To his often unrecognised credit his stance against the IRA has always been tough (and for that he has earned the organisation's condemnation) but latterly he has made direct appeals to both the IRA and Unionist militants to abandon their violent campaigns and join in a pan-national attempt to solve the North's festering divisions. Here was an indication of restructured republicanism, one which allowed no ambiguity about the tyranny of gunmen, and reaffirmed his country's commitment to enforce law against terrorism. 'Violence to achieve political ends,' he says, 'has no place in Western democracies.'

Haughey's new air of gravitas may spring from the profound recognition that in his 65th year he knows there is a limit on any time left to prove he is more than a mischief-making power-seeker and intolerant grandee. In fact this veteran trouper has jumped so many rings that statesmanship remains the only goal outstanding, the ultimate challenge to establish the honour of that 1979 intention about working towards just and lasting peace in Northern Ireland.

Even so in Dublin the old gamey stories about him still survive. The best, of course, concern the popular myths surrounding his activities as a ladies' man, and while it may have been a silver teapot that he took to the once most powerful woman in the world, it is said to have been a genuine crocodile handbag that he gave to another woman he admired. The tale goes that after a tiff in a restaurant she walked out and flung it into the River Liffey, whereupon Charlie rolled up his trouser legs and waded in after it.

The hell-raising days may be over now, but the eyes still glint rather than cosily twinkle. 'The Taoiseach's national standing has increased since his decision not to give any more major press interviews,' one aide observed some years ago. Was this the strategy of cynicism, the tactics of a man rendered untouchable by his scuffling apparatchiks? No one should under-estimate Haughey The Enigma, Haughey The Transformed.

15

SCENES
Dail Sketch

IT IS the first afternoon of parliamentary business following the Easter recess and the Taoiseach is taking questons for oral answer in the Dail. Through the cupola steely shards of sunlight are hardening the general brightness of the Chamber, heightening the lapis blue of the carpet with its gold border of Celtic scrolls and adding to the buttocked shine on the brown leather seats. Up in the public gallery signs demanding silence and forbidding any applause convey something of the emotional gravity of Irish politics. Even from this distance the visitor can see that Charles Haughey has lost the richly veined complexion which once distinguished his appearance. In its place there is a hint of a healthier, seafaring tan which, since serious illness some years ago, denotes the bibulous days are over. Looking down into the Chamber from here it is impossible to detect the notorious flint in the eyes, but their hooded lids and the natural downturn of the mouth give an imperious, inscrutable expression. And if it is true that the face is an index of the mind then on that premise alone Mr Haughey is the mandarin of Irish politics. One notices his hands particularly – unexpectedly slender, artistic and pale, these are the hands of a man who likes to consider himself at home in elegant company, and on this afternoon he uses them in restrained, sophisticated gestures to emphasise his Government's commitment to Peter Brooke's initiative on Northern Ireland. But there is also something about their groomed manner which smacks of self-delight; an affirmation

151

of his belief that while Charles J. Haughey is a politician of the world his fellow parliamentarians are still trapped in the province of small ideas.

The Opposition parties are seizing on the phrase 'all party talks' in Mr Brooke's communiqué to demand their inclusion in Dublin's round table delegation. Taoiseach Haughey coolly dismisses the notion, insisting that only the Irish Government will conduct the talks on behalf of the Republic. To do otherwise would simply complicate a complex and intricate framework for discussion which has already taken years of patient and visionary endeavour to achieve. The Opposition are unimpressed. Has the Government learned nothing from the past? asks one deputy. Initiatives like Sunningdale and Hillsborough have run into trouble before because key people were not included in the negotiations . . . A sense of scorn is now enveloping the Taoiseach who disposes of the question by reminding the Chamber that he is a student of history and as such the lessons of history always command his respect.

But still the Opposition are dissatisfied. Both Labour and Fine Gael demand to know whether the Progressive Democrats (the junior partners in the coalition) are to be represented at the talks. Long ago, however, Mr Haughey perfected the art of lofty evasion. The Government and only the Government will conduct the talks for Ireland, he repeats. And then as a sop to this fractious exchange he discloses his intention that the other parties in the Dail be kept 'fully informed and to the greatest extent involved in some way yet to be decided'. Like a company chairman delivering a board report, he speaks without intonation in a hurried and rather dusty voice. He is asked to elaborate and suddenly the honed blade of short temper cuts through the semantic rigmarole. This, he says in reference to the Brooke initiative, is a big, important occasion which could lead to an historic opportunity and he cannot understand why deputies wish to stir things up with petty, party differences. 'Is that what you're at?' he snaps. 'Is that what you're at?'

Some ten minutes later Sean Treacy, Ceann Comhairle (Speaker), warns that the questions are becoming over-windy and over-long, an implication that only a certain degree of windiness is acceptable in Irish political debate. Asked yet again to clarify his position the Taoiseach re-applies his caustic strategy. No doubt if he recited the Apostles' Creed, he says, the deputy in question would still ask him to identify his religion.

The air of statesmanship has settled only recently on Charles Haughey who in March 1991 made what may come to be regarded as the seminal speech of his long career. At the annual conference of his party, Fianna Fail, he urged bemused delegates to rise to the challenge of an Irish perestroika, pledging: 'We are committed to a new era of social consensus . . . Our ambition is to create a new progressive, prosperous and enlightened society that excels in the quality of life and the services it provides for its citizens, and that belongs among the advanced nations of Europe . . .'

But in the Dail that Wednesday, more than one month after the revelation of that new vision, there were many who wondered if the Great Progressive of Irish Society wasn't still the Great Oppor- tunist they had witnessed and fought so many times before. Here is a man whose use of absolute power defines his understanding of democracy, and who, through its application, has survived more attempted political coups and fiascos than any other leader in the European Community. A man of unyielding ambition and tightly packed containment, Mr Haughey is the only member that day who reads from his papers without the aid of spectacles. At the end of the session he moves from the Chamber on cat's feet, a Taoiseach who leaves no tracks.

FIANNA FAIL has nearly always secured the ballot box with the rural vote, for out in the country its diehards still regard themselves as inheritors of de Valera's Soldiers of Destiny. If Fine Gael, taste- fully suited in the style of the well-educated professional classes, represents the quality grocer come to town then Fianna Fail repre- sents not only the upstart supermarket tycoon but also his father, the grocer who has stayed shrewdly in the country. He is the gombeen man, the prosperous merchant among small farmers whose local shop and bar are ever open, covering all contingencies from birth to death. In his arched and pillared *palazzo gombini*, he presides as everybody's indispensable middleman offering nappies and headstones, plus unswerving loyalty to the Fianna Fail machine.

But what is Ireland buying if it votes for Fine Gael? One of the country's three conservative parties, its problem is that it is per- ceived by the young not only as middle-class but old middle-class. In fact there is a saying that while Fianna Fail is rarely out of power, Fine Gael, in its own way, is rarely out of power either. The party's members and supporters wield an influence which has more to do with the inherited social confidence of generations of 'good schooling' than with any obvious wealth. So, to many, it is still regarded as a kind of freemasonry owning a code of speech and behaviour and, in many instances, adhering to a right-wing hierarchy, something a former leader, Garret FitzGerald, sought to change.

Dessie O'Malley's Progressive Democrats, the youngest of the right-wing movements, was formed in 1985, by this somewhat Thatcherite Limerick lawyer who had been in government as a Fianna Fail Minister until his not infrequent altercations with Mr Haughey finally forced his exit from the party. Mary Harney, one of the Republic's most articulate and gifted politicians, defected also, joining with O'Malley to form the PDs, the only one of Ireland's major parties not to have been born of the country's historic conflicts. Instead its *raison d'être* was the social and economic problems of the day and, though numerically weak, it has been an effective junior partner in the coalition Government established in 1989, urging it to adopt a more conciliatory tone with the North, placing brakes on the kind of preferential trading treatment of which the mighty Goodman meat empire availed itself, and generally confronting reality. Dessie O'Malley's speeches on the need for constitutional change are widely considered to be among the most persuasive in a historic debate. Still there is a piquancy in the image of Dessie and Charlie locked together in an expedient embrace. Bad blood boiled between them for years, O'Malley's uneasiness with the Fianna Fail leader's bullish style dating from the gun-running trial in which Haughey was implicated in the early 1970s. Later, on the issue of public performance, O'Malley attemped to oust the multi-millionaire as party supremo but failed.

Perhaps the Labour Party's greatest success in Ireland was its endorsement of Mary Robinson as a candidate for the Presidency in May 1990. Her eventual triumph as a contender of the Left (she was also supported by the Workers' Party) was another example of leader Dick Spring's alert sensitivity to the nuances of change in Irish society, a subtle undercurrent scarcely recognised by the two main parties. The previous year it was also Dick Spring, another astute lawyer – this time from Kerry – who attacked Charles Haughey for acting against the Constitution when he sought to govern without a clear mandate. Today Spring has set himself the onerous challenge of turning Labour into the second largest party in the country, replacing the founder James Connolly's old aspirations to a 32-county workers' republic with the more realistic acknowledgement that a mixed economy is what the young electorate desires. The haul towards doubling the party's support and gaining between 30 and 40 seats in the Dail will be a long, tough struggle but Spring, still in his mid-forties, is young and commanding enough to see it achieved. 'There is something new out there,' said one of the delegates at Labour's annual conference in March 1991. 'We can sense it in our very bones.' Just less than 12 months earlier, on a fine summer day in Dublin's Merrion Square, Dick Spring had said much the same thing in the course of a buffet lunch. Only then he was launching Mary Robinson's crusading voyage towards the Presidential Mansion in Phoenix Park. Setting out now on a new journey, here is a man of serious hunches.

16

VOICES
Gay Byrne

FOR MORE THAN 20 years the currency of Gay Byrne's life has been the stealthy power of secrets. The confidences are entrusted to him not in the dark, whispering corners of the world but out on the airwaves; ripped into the bald light of a television studio where an audience sits mesmerised by the skittish or sobbing disclosures of its own collective soul. Stretching over almost three decades Byrne has remained Ireland's superlative communicator, a conduit through which flows a nation's exuberant gift for hilarity, its concealed grievances and pain, its neglected aspirations and its anger. One century from now any social historian, casting back to learn the mood and pre-occupations of Dublin today, might find no more accurate gauge than the play-backs of Gay Byrne's daily radio programme for the national station, and his compelling series, *The Late Late Show* from RTE on a Friday night.

There is a mercurial quality to Byrne which has secured his catch-all presence on the Irish scene. Joshing, mischievous, painstakingly sympathetic or acerbic, he is always fluently informed enough to expose the troublesome nerve or demand answers to the kind of uncomfortable questions which have authority metaphorically jumping out of windows. In the general flabbiness of chat shows it seems fanciful to describe Gay Byrne as a phenomenon but that word is not at all far-fetched. In Britain and on the Continent certainly there is no one in a similar position who comes close to his unremitting skills at excavating merriment or hideously raw self-knowledge

157

from those sitting in the studio's brown swivel chairs, or clenching the receiver at the other end of a telephone line. Within 15 minutes he can dismiss, cajole, deride, applaud and comfort, assured now that the top ratings are his, and the reason is straightforward. In a nation which fought heroically for independence, then rationed some of its fresh freedom with new autocratic controls, Gay Byrne allowed himself to become the voice of the agitated, the man who dared others to trample on taboos.

Through all of this, of course, his professional hunger for riveting material has played a major part. Byrne never set out to change his country's attitudes, but by arriving back in Dublin in the mid-Sixties, after a successful career at Granada Television in Manchester, he was poised to achieve kudos because, in any circumstances, he was an accomplished, urbane and sharp-witted broadcaster. More significantly, though, RTE had just been born without the encumbrance of a code of behaviour tied around its neck. 'We were living with the legacy of de Valera,' Byrne reflects. 'This was Ireland, the land of absolutes, of sacred cows and Gaelic culture. And we stepped in, a new television crowd that was young, arrogant and pushy. We didn't feel constrained by the sanctions and moral diktats which governed radio, and because many of the early programme-makers came from abroad, they didn't feel restricted by the shibboleths in Irish society.

'So there was this upstart Gay Byrne on television, talking about homosexuality to the family. In God's name what was the country coming to . . .' Byrne himself still muses on his audacity with astonishment. And, like anybody dealing with contentious matters in the media, Gaybo's *Late Late Show* came under fearsome pressure from the hierarchy and other authorities to drop certain subjects. Tenaciously the team held its ground but it was in 1966 that it first knew it had really scored. During the programme an amiable woman called Eileen Fox disclosed that she had worn nothing in bed on her wedding night. Across the Irish sea this was the Swinging Decade and Byrne, exploiting Britain's noisy raciness, wouldn't let the matter rest, but it was banter not prurience that governed the oul' chat. Within minutes, however, 'incensed respectability' had jammed the switchboard, demanding that 'this dirty programme' be abolished immediately. An even heavier onslaught assailed the RTE telephones when Byrne raised the issue of women's liberation. But then the outpouring was so

158

overwhelmingly supportive that any uncomprehending men who weighed in on the attack found themselves submerged beneath the pain of angry sisterhood.

Walled up for generations, the anguish and frustrations were suddenly – on radio and television – dismantling their prison brick by brick. The ironies in all this are considerable. Gay Byrne is no great feminist yet he enabled the women's movement to happen in Ireland. If anything he is that most curious of creatures, a conventional man who has radicalised his environment. Conformist, if slightly Puckish, in appearance, he is, to some, irritatingly cynical, glib and sarcastic, and occasionally mocking in the company of the great. But he has, as they say, proved you can be a good Catholic and talk about contraceptives on television. 'When we came along sex was certainly not discussed in public, and because it wasn't it was almost presumed that it didn't exist.' There were many times, he remembers, when his job seemed on the line, although the late Eamonn Andrews, chairman of RTE Authority, was one of his most committed defenders. 'That wasn't widely known but he did stick out against the establishment for our kind of vigorous television.'

At first hearing Byrne's daily radio show seems an innocuous mix of filleted music, soft current affairs and a bit of inconsequential jaw with the listeners. But in between the patter and the jolly anecdotes it can also peel back the silence of devastating secrets. In the mid-Eighties a schoolgirl died alone in childbirth near a religious grotto at Granard in Longford, an incident which subsequently revealed once again the terrified ignorance and dread of sexual discovery which still controls so many lives. Letters poured in to the Dublin studio and, without identifying the correspondents, Byrne read out the tales of suppressed but unmitigated misery; stories of vandalised innocence, of disowned or hidden illegitimate children; stories of dreadful suffering often caused by others' hypocrisy, and the utter contorting loneliness of burying a powerful secret forever. But here it was again, that shaming realisation on the part of the public that Gay Byrne was only the caretaker of such heart-wrenching intimacies because there was no one else in whom the victims could confide.

Byrne believes that Mary Robinson's Presidency, although symbolic, marks a turning point in Irish affairs. 'It caught the establishment on one leg,' he says. 'And now there are signs that

159

they are putting the two feet down and running to keep up with the rest of the land.' Yet for any country defined by the sharpness of recent history Ireland's dilemma now concerns how much of its past it wishes to lose. 'I believe there is a deep spirituality in Irish people and that has to be respected,' he says. There is also, he feels, an increasing rift between Dublin and the remainder of the country: 'A sense that Dublin is far too centrist. Mind you, Dublin is not alone in that. It was true of Thatcher's rule at Westminster. But there are those who will tell you that we are being governed by the Doheny and Nesbitt school of economists [*a reference to a supposedly opinion-forming pub on Baggot Street*]. This crew is said to run the economy rather than the nation, and there might, indeed, be some truth in that.'

Twenty years ago, he says, the three key issues which dominated the debating arena were the Provisional IRA and Northern Ireland, the Gaelic language, and sex. 'Today people are wearying of discussing the first. And the second, the Gaelic language, has lost its vehement supporters and protesters to acquire just the moderate level of interest it deserves. But sex is as tumultuous as ever.' The proof of this came early in 1991; in fact just at a time when Gay Byrne feared that life was becoming tamer and there might not be too many hush-hush topics left to brandish before the nation. Suddenly Dublin was caught up in the fiasco of Virgin condoms. 'Most people, I think, couldn't believe the hierarchy were making this fuss over contraceptives in 1991.' But even so the extreme protests illustrated the lingering tensions between the old and the new in Irish society. 'Here, in effect, was a battle of wills: modern Ireland with its European ambitions lined up against the conservative element which feels it might be losing its grip.' Whatever the outcome of that particular war Gay Byrne's confessional role is fixed. Sex, after all, is what keep us going . . . keeps us in disarray.

17

THEMES
The Easter Rising

NOTHING MORE defined the dilemma of this small country in transition than the 75th anniversary of the Easter Rising, those six days in Dublin which nailed the world's attention to a hapless bunch of patriots seeking freedom from colonial rule. To celebrate the rebellion with the full panoply of state was, in many eyes, to risk the event being perceived as an endorsement of today's Provisional IRA. Yet to ignore it was to abandon history and the imperative of nationhood, thereby creating a kind of cultural denial which terrorists would in any case exploit.

Against this unease the Irish Government chose to honour the heroes of 1916 on Easter Sunday 1991 in Dublin with an event of simple brevity: no parade, no speeches, no chance for political opportunism from any quarter. Instead the occasion was marked by 'military ceremonial' consisting of two army bands playing traditional airs, a guard of honour inspected by President Mary Robinson, a reading of the Proclamation drawn up by the rebels and the Provisional Government in that cathartic Easter week, and the hoisting of the national flag above the GPO, the building held by the patriots during the insurrection. Taoiseach Charles Haughey attended, along with leaders of the opposition parties, and the whole affair, enacted in O'Connell Street, was concluded in less than an hour.

And that would have been the end of it had the Government not run into competition from those who believed its 'static display' of

161

neglect was not only niggardly but indicative of a loss of nerve. 'We argued very strongly that the rejection of the Rising because of its connection with men of violence was a red herring,' says the Dublin artist Robert Ballagh, one of the leading activists in the Reclaim the Spirit of Easter 1916 Committeee which one week after the Government's event arranged an alternative and far more vigorous commemoration in the form of a pageant of theatrical and carnival activities through the centre of Dublin. 'The fact is that the politicians know full well that they have failed to meet the aspirations of the Proclamation,' argues Ballagh. 'And so any public reading of it is something to be gone through as quickly as possible.' Although Ballagh's committee failed to find the support of any national party leaders (and received no official funds for its festivities), the artist is not alone in his contention that the Proclamation has been betrayed. Dick Spring, leader of the Labour Party, has consistently maintained that it is not possible to talk truthfully about a society that cherishes all children of the nation equally when education is increasingly a privilege, and not a right, and when quick access to health care is a function of income. 'When the average income of women is two-thirds of the average income of men,' he argues, 'how can I talk of "equal rights and opportunity"?' And, in a country which facilitates the death of marriage but refuses to accept the right of remarriage, it is impossible, in Spring's view, to speak of a society that 'guarantees religious and civil liberty'.

Yet that sentiment is unequivocally enshrined in the dramatic and emotional language of the Proclamation which was signed by Thomas J. Clarke, Sean MacDiarmada, Padraig Pearse, James Connelly, Thomas MacDonagh, Eamonn Ceannt and Joseph Plunkett:

'Irishmen and Irishwomen: In the name of God and of dead generations from which she received her rich tradition of nationhood, Ireland, through us, summons her children to her flag and strikes for her freedom . . . The Irish Republic is entitled to, and hereby claims, the allegiance of every Irishman and Irishwoman. The Republic guarantees religious and civil liberty, equal rights and equal opportunities to all its citizens, and declares its resolve to pursue the happiness and prosperity of the whole nation and of all its parts, cherishing all the children of the nation equally.'

But while Ballagh would argue that the vast majority of Irish people, and Dubliners in particular, remain unconvinced by the revisionist historians who seek to exorcise the spirit of 1916, there is at last a realisation that 'all the children of the nation' do not feel comfortable with the ethos of the Easter Rising. The Republic's minority Protestant community finds little identification with nationalist martyrs. Now, for the first time, its alienation is being recognised by those determined to transform Ireland into a pluralist community. 'It is time to leave the bitter past to history and to look at the future,' said Charles Haughey in his 1991 speech defining his version of Irish perestroika. 'Our ambition is to create a new progressive, prosperous and enlightened society that excels in the quality of life and the services it provides for its citizens, and that belongs among the advanced nations of Europe.'

But the furore over the Taoiseach's proposal to provide condoms for people from the age of 16 illustrated precisely the lingering handicap of a country which had replaced colonial domination with Catholic control. This modest attempt to update the Republic's meagre birth control laws exposed the continuing readiness of bishops and their fundamentalist prompters to exploit the Rome ticket on political and social issues. That fate was, perhaps, inevitable, given that Ireland, on gaining independence, was considerably unprepared and ill equipped for the intricacies and challenges that the sudden gift of power imposed. Dr Noel Browne, one of the few political intellectuals in Irish life, has observed that a nation which, for centuries, had endured the violent, repressive destruction of its own unique ethos and nationhood found it impossible to emerge with its political self-esteem and national identity undamaged:

'In 1922, finally liberated from colonial oppression, we were totally inexperienced in the exercise of power in a popular democracy. In the majority an embittered, illiterate peasant people, unprepared for the sophisticated complexities of our new freedom, we shed the oppressive restrictions of British imperial power to slide, willingly, into the secure, welcoming, anti-democratic totalitarian cocoon of Rome rule.'

In time, he argued, the social effect was the replacement of the British by an equally insensitive and uncaring Irish (and mostly Dublin) ruling class which, in Dr Browne's view, included the de Valera dynasty, and in a contemporary context the millionaire circles of such politicians as Charles Haughey, John Bruton, Albert

Reynolds, and industrialists like Michael Smurfit and Tony O'Reilly. But Dr Browne also traces the dependence on Rome back to the post-Reformation era. Having by then lost much of its control of Western Europe, Rome fought desperately to hold on to power in Ireland. 'The peasant Catholic Irish were encouraged by Rome to resist the only aristocracy they had; they were bad land-lords anyway and were both Protestant and English. So did the Irish freedom movement merge to make nationalism and religion fight a common cause.'

Haughey's objection to the orthodox bishops' teaching on the subject of condoms marked a historic break with Vatican domina-tion. For until that moment – since the formation of the State in 1922 – poor Irish domestic life had revolved around a loyalty to Rome rather than to the Republic. During that Easter of 1916, however, those few thousand warriors who had waged the Rising had done so without the Church's blessing. In military terms the Dublin insurgency failed abysmally; its only success was the bitter windfall of martyrs to the Cause as Britain, after a series of secret court-martials, set about executing the 15 leaders, including James Connelly and Padraig Pearse, at the rate of two or three a day. With those deaths the mood of the people changed from antagonism towards the rebels because of the damage and injury suffered by innocent civilians to one of patriotic fervour. The flame of nationalism had been ignited as six years later the British withdrew from 26 of Ireland's 32 counties.

Yet for all its bravery and impassioned conviction, the Easter insurgency was a ramshackle affair, a hopeless adventure against the 'greatest military power on earth'. The newspaper coverage of the time conveys something of the futility and pathos of the con-spirators' tactics. The GPO itself – their greatest seizure – was barricaded from inside with 'bags, papers and all available books'. On 10 May 1916, the *Irish Independent* recorded: 'In one of the street encounters a rebel and a soldier rushed at one another. The soldier was a Dublin man drafted in to help quell the rising. "My God, Tom, is this where I find you?" he said. "Run for your life!" The brother turned and fled. This was not the only case where families found themselves fighting on opposing sides.'

Some inkling of the sudden manner in which the whole event erupted and its lack of popular endorsement or awareness is apparent in the following vignette taken from the *Dublin Evening*

Herald, also of 10 May 1916: 'A lady on her way to a distant part of the country arrived in Dublin on Easter Monday and was passing along Henry Street near the PO about two o'clock when without the remotest suspicion of the Rising she found herself in the midst of a battle. For her safety and protection some Volunteers ordered her to take refuge in the PO. She thereupon entered the building where she remained until 11.30 p.m. on Friday next . . . Eventually she and another girl were put out over a wall at the back, and made their way over the debris of Henry Street between blazing and tottering houses and in the midst of a hurricane of bullets, to a place of safety where they were hospitably treated till Wednesday morning.'

Since the Troubles began in Northern Ireland in 1968 atrocity has stained the name of Republicanism in the South, and yet for some people – a minority, but still enough for it to matter – such committed viciousness has not destroyed the ambiguity felt about those who personally absolve their crimes by claiming they are the inheritors of the men of 1916.

But in 1987 something happened in the opulent Dublin neighbourhood of Foxrock which cleared muddled perceptions. Like so many victims in Derry or Belfast, the dentist John O'Grady will always bear the physical scars of his abduction from his father-in-law's desirable home by a bunch of criminals led by Dessie O'Hare, a terrorist whose insubordination caused him to be disowned by both the Provisional IRA and the Irish National Liberation Army, and whose inventory of assassinations is thought to cover more than 20 names. The little finger on each of O'Grady's hands was hacked off at the second joint by a chisel and hammer, and then with singular callousness the kidnappers made their prisoner cauterise his own wounds using a hot knife. Behind that monstrous image is the venom of gangland, and to link it as Dessie O'Hare – now serving a prison sentence in Portlaoise – unswervingly did to the pursuit of a united Ireland is to desecrate the very notion of heroic ideals.

No one witnessing the impressive dignity with which Dr Austin Darragh described his son-in-law's torturers, on release, could have failed to understand that family's message: patriotism gained by others' blood is civilisation's downward spiral into barbarity. For the very sake of Ireland, any perilous equivocation over paramilitary activities must cease.

But without advocating violence Robert Ballagh espouses Republicanism out of a belief that modern Ireland has become a country with no vision of itself. 'Look at Dublin,' he says. 'The bureaucrats and local authorities have destroyed it with, among other things, the most disastrous road plans ever foisted on a city. The scheme for two motorways has been on the go for 20 years and still nothing. Meanwhile some of the most handsome buildings have been bulldozed to make way for Third World-style shopping centres.' Ballagh also contends that although emigration is not official policy in Ireland, it serves a useful purpose for the ruling establishment, and therefore is never really addressed. 'It exports dissent, talent and creativity.'

However, the young Dublin novelist Dermot Bolger is typical of that generation born in the late Fifties which feels no compulsion to hark back to 1916 for its ethnic and cultural credentials. 'For me Ireland began somewhere around 1945. In Dublin during part of the Seventies there was something akin to an economic miracle and my generation was perhaps the only one which did not have to leave the country. Today, the situation is very different and while it is sad, the positive aspect of present emigration is that our young people are to Ireland what champagne is to France.' Bolger believes the Nineties will be good for Ireland, and for Dublin in particular, because he is among those who endorse the view that the election of Mary Robinson to the Presidency (although a symbolic role) marks a turning point towards radicalism in Irish politics. 'Dublin is a very special capital city in that it is still very rural in parts. But the young who remain, and who return, are energising it and broadening it into a European dimension. Dublin in the next decade will gain enormously in maturity and achievement.'

This entrusting of the future to Europe – instead of using the past to intimidate the future – cannot now be dismissed by any senior Dublin politician. The prospect of a still more integrated Europe is finally widening the pinched horizons of Ireland both North and South. Mr Haughey, during the Fianna Fail Ard-Fheis (policy conference) in Dublin in 1991, said: 'I am increasingly convinced that it is in the context of the new European Union that we will find a solution to the centuries-old, deeply-embedded problem that still persists in Northern Ireland, and that continues to exact a terrible price for our failure to find a solution. Before the end of this decade, all Irish men and women, North and South, will be fellow citizens of a united Europe. There will be no real border between North and South; the ECU will be our common currency, and we will live under the same kind of economic and financial regimes. In effect the people of Ireland will be united in a united Europe. This is the political reality, and we should now, North and South, begin to prepare ourselves for it.'

Taoiseach Haughey, assuming the unaccustomed mantle of benign elder statesman, was urging his followers to recognise that the overwhelming impact of European political, economic and monetary union would make the partition between North and South (always unnatural) irrelevant. Was he, in effect, preparing the party faithful, de Valera's Soldiers of Destiny, for the kind of constitutional change which would remove those clauses defining the 'national territory' as all of Ireland? Whether motivated by opportunism or by a real if belated commitment to a radical philosophy, Charles Haughey's new voice did seem to splinter the united front of nationalist romance still preached and practised by some influential politicians in Ireland.

'If the whole island and all the people on it are to benefit from the dynamism of European Union, an all-Ireland approach to all sectors of economic policy and investment should begin now,' he said. 'It is imperative that we should now, together, North and South, prepare to secure the greatest possible advantage from the new situation to our mutual benefit. This concept of mutual benefit should become our new guiding principle, North and South. It is the one which can inspire a radical change in outlook in all areas of life on this island.'

Within a few weeks of this oration came the accouncement by the Northern Ireland Secretary Peter Brooke of formal political talks with all sides on the festering wounds of Northern Ireland: a breakthrough, after months of patient listening and talking and sometimes near despair, which the Irish Government described as a 'historic chance for reconciliation between the two traditions of this island', a statement which clearly reinforced the official decision to mark patriotic anniversaries in only the most nominal way. Now those talks have collapsed, but in the South, it might be that Robert Ballagh's real success has been the return of 1916 to the agenda for social debate. Dubliners are a garrulous breed but very often the verbal cunning and razor wit belong to the tricks of a people used to hiding things, both from the enemy and themselves.

On sensitive issues they can be reticent for as long as is possible. Then, when winkled out, they joke, a method of keeping difficult or painful facts at bay. But in the new Dublin there needs to be open discussion on the very nature of heroism today, and on whether internecine carnage can ever be justified. In the new Ireland there can be no room for the sterile politics of tribal and religious grievance. The last 20 years have exposed the wickedness and disaster of constantly nourishing old sores, for the ruling tragedies of the entire landscape have been the twin strains of virulent nationalism. Now, in both Dublin and Belfast, the only important battle left is for time, that most precious commodity which, too often, both sides have stolen from their children.

18

VOICES
Patrick Kavanagh

BETWEEN LEESON STREET and Baggot Street Bridge, where the wind whacks the old snug smells of beer and tobacco right out from under the nostrils, there is a bench on the banks of the Grand Canal, with a plaque on it dedicated to a poet from his friends. Sixty odd paces away on the opposite side of the canal there is another bench where the man himself is seated in bronze contemplation of his giant's feet. In a city which loves to make its geniuses immobile this is a more sympathetic and appropriate memorial than many. And yet the lads in the plaques sector of Public Works might just as well have slapped a brass plate on the bottom of an upturned bar stool for Patrick Kavanagh used drinking stations as if they were intensive care units devised for him alone.

Being a fierce individual for rows Kavanagh was evicted frequently from these premises yet that was just part of the pageant, the climax of a virtuoso performance of vivid lyricism and blather accompanied by limitless imbibing. Suddenly his gangling bulk – 'great roots of hands' – 'a voice like coal sliding down a chute' – would threaten to reduce a pub to smithereens. But although proprietors might have thrown him out more times than they can recall, hardly any of them found such rough exits altered their friendship with the man. 'He lived a long decomposition, etherealised at intervals into poems,' wrote the English literary academic Hugh Kenner in his study of modern Irish writers, *A Colder Eye*. In fact Kavanagh died at the age of 63 in 1967. Physically awkward, he smashed things unwittingly whether drink was in him or not. This tendency he attributed to the 'destructive power of the poet' but it had more to do with a rural clumsiness which hung about him like a faithful, mis-shapen overcoat. The son of a shoemaker who farmed on the side in Inniskeen, County Monaghan, Kavanagh grew up hearing everyone in the family scold him: 'You broke everything on the farm, except the crowbar. And you bent that.'

The bench memorials, however, provide a valuable reminder of a complex man whose visual gaucheness masked a sharp intelligence and made him the butt of many a patronising Dublin joke. It was on the bank that Kavanagh would sit daily and 'let the water lap idly on the shores of my mind'. By 1956 he had already defined his own throne for posterity with the lines:

> O commemorate me with no hero-courageous tomb
> But just a canal-bank seat for the passer by.

Kavanagh's purpose in life, he said, was to have no purpose. Such confessed indifference diminished a man who cared passionately, brilliantly and bitterly about his talent, but the immodesty of this noisy lack of ego exacted a heavy sum. It ensured his dismissal by the literary king-makers of his day while the perpetual, and often liquid, vigour of his conversation confirmed for many a Dubliner the self-destructive notion that the artist who isn't intoxicated isn't the authentic article.

Nevertheless Kavanagh's ebullience was devious, a disguise to conceal shyness and a delicate imagination, and what started him off on poetry wasn't wicked old Dublin at all but the cruel, rural texture of his native County Monaghan. Here was hard, grey stony land which strangled every single living thing it encountered. In his most desolate poem, *The Great Hunger*, which some years ago was translated into a theatrical piece by Tom MacIntyre at the Abbey Theatre and then the Edinburgh Festival, Kavanagh describes with aching accuracy the inertia, the tight, sour fears and sexual repressions of an impoverished and barbarous life. Its bleak bachelor hero, Patrick Maguire, is praised by his mother for making 'a field his bride', the denial of marriage being a complex and vicious form of birth control in a primitive community nailed to the land:

> He stands in the doorway of the mind,
> October creaks the rotted mattress,

170

The bedposts fall. No hope.
No lust.

In reality Kavanagh only just escaped a similar fate, marrying late and living out the remaining years in Dublin with his craggy, unpoetic Katherine in a certain cantankerous bliss. Poor for most of his days, he scrounged his way around the city earning pints at different bars through sharpening up the scene, goading other mavericks like the columnist Myles na Gopaleen and the writer Brendan Behan, and exploiting the role of peasant occasionally inspired to poetic utterance, a 'country gobshite' shielding the mystical wonder of his soul against any city-slicker's cunning.

Ironically *The Great Hunger* became the poem he liked least. What displeased him most was its lack of objectivity, its obvious wounds and howling pain, its ranting fight to break the umbilical cord with the earth, and the tyrannous cries of mothering. And yet that poem remains a rooted metaphor for Ireland, narrow hamlet and brazen town alike. As for the Dublin Paddy Kavanagh knew, it has altered substantially in physical terms, but emotionally maybe not so much. Still, the very mention of the man's name is enough to cause a rumpus in the letters column of the *Irish Times*. Not very long ago the Public Works Department arbitrarily sought to replace Paddy Kavanagh's canal bench with one dedicated to the composer of light music, Percy French. The thunder of fury descended forcing the PW to seek out enough funds to remove the original bench, which was in acute need of repair, and plant two new ones, one to the memory of French, as intended, and the other, on the opposite bank, recalling the commemoration by his friends of Kavanagh, the man regarded by many scholars now as one of the most influential Irish poets since Yeats. Since then there has followed the sculptor John Coll's splendid evocation of the poet either dozing or composing on another bench, his hat at his side, a statue provided by ICI to mark Dublin's year as European City of Culture in 1991. And, as if in reparation for the dinginess that had overtaken this corner through neglect, the authorities have cleaned the water and restocked it with fish while Bord Failte (the Irish Tourist Board) – supported by various commercial enterprises in the vicinity – have landscaped the stretch into something pleasurable, something which becomes, in Kavanagh's own words, 'leafy-with-love/greeny at the heart of summer'.

So, almost 25 years after his death, Kavanagh's cultural importance is being reassessed. The literary status which eluded him in life is now being wrapped around his memory by an international following. Would such deference impress the 'ploughman-about-town'? Probably not. Like Beckett, Kavanagh hated the élitist bleatings of academic hangers-on. 'A poet merely states the position and does not care whether his words change anything or not,' he scoffed. He believed, though, that tragedy was undeveloped comedy, and he knew also how to play poetry for engaging self-derision. As the man said, while buttressing the bar . . .

> The main thing is to continue
> To walk Parnassus right into the sunset
> Detached in love where pygmies
> Cannot pin you
> To the ground like Gulliver. So
> Good luck and cheers.

19

SCENES
Tallaght

AT THE TOP of Kiltipper Road there are brambles springing over the high stone wall, and lower along on the left large gates mark the entrance to the community dump ground set discreetly a quarter of a mile in from the road over raggedy mountain fields. Down below lie the rooftops of Tallaght, uniform lids on pale box houses which have multiplied in 20 years to accommodate 70,000 people, most of them 'blow-ins' from the suburbs seeking their first married home, or else whole families decanted from Dublin's inner dereliction.

Tallaght, resting in a hollow of the Dublin mountains, means the Valley of the Plague and no name could be more painful in a country with an inherited folk memory of the Famine when pestilence further mocked the agonies of the impoverished. But neither could it be more damning to these newer folk fighting against a tide of bureaucratic indifference, and tight-lipped bigotry, to establish an independent sense of self-esteem. Dating from pre-Viking days, Tallaght was once the trading point for local agriculture and its old village still acts as the inextinguishable pulse of today's sprawling neighbourhoods, a mixture of concrete-rendered local authority housing and privately built homes intersected now by dual carriageways and industrial estates. Johnson & Johnson are here and so are Irish Biscuits, Reckitt Colman and Glenabbey Textiles, and The Square, one of those dazzlingly seductive retailing malls, has recently opened, inspired by the American trick of turning

173

shopping into a leisure pursuit. But here also are Mrs Bolger's cakes and scones, the fluffy, creamy home baking of a matriarch now in her seventies whose refreshments first nourished old Tallaght long ago and now find a wider following among today's grazing consumers.

The ancient *Book of Invasions* provides an early reference to Tallaght, recording a settlement of a tribe called the Parthalons, descended from the Greeks, who were afflicted by a ferocious disease which in one week alone claimed the lives of 4,000 women and 1,000 men. Within a short period 9,000 victims were dead and the Parthalons became extinct. In 1951 there were 350 people living in the village whose only widely known features offered a furious vision of heaven and hell. In the eighth century Tallaght was the site of an influential monastery established by Abbot Maelruain, a harsh fundamentalist who founded one of the most repressive sects, the Culdees, in early Church history. Centuries later, and with brazen disregard for any admonishing Culdee ghost lurking in the hillsides, a rabble of high-society bucks from Dublin established the Hell Fire Club on top of Tallaght's Montpelier Hill. Built in 1720, this strange bleak edifice was well out of reach of prying wives and authority and there, in what was originally intended as a hunting lodge, the gang caroused until one night the roof blew off revealing, according to rumour, the devil in all his combustible grandeur. Never had the gentlemen's horses and traps careered down those rocky roads at more demented speed, and to this day the Hell Fire Club remains, a haunting ruin perched on a summit like a commemorative cairn, visible for miles around.

By the middle of the 1990s Tallaght is expected to have 100,000 residents, and like those of today theirs will be a story of common endeavour and defiant optimism in the face of outside parsimony and prejudice.

To begin, then, at the recent beginning. In 1972 the County Dublin Development Plan identified Tallaght, along with Blanchardstown, Lucan and Clondalkin, as a major growth location which would accommodate the significant natural increase in the population of Dublin, plus those continuing to migrate to the capital. But like all such brave, grand schemes that are based on pouring maximum population into low-cost housing, Tallaght became the Irish archetype of mutton-headed planning. Thousands of people, mostly with young families, were pitched out eight miles from the city with no amenities save the shelter of their raw, new houses. 'There were no buses, no roads except rocky boreens, no shops and no phone boxes,' says Bob Byrne, long regarded as an inspirational member of Tallaght Community Council. 'It's difficult to imagine how bleak it was. I was among the first influx, just married and delighted to be setting up house in such a lovely setting. But in some ways we were as badly off as refugees in a transit camp. The trouble was we were so far out we seemed to come under the mantle of no-one. Families were being given the key in Dublin, then lorried in and left sometimes for days with no lighting, no heating, no furniture even. The planners simply hadn't thought through the consequences of turning a village overnight into a town.'

Many times the teething problems threatened to turn septic, some of the new neighbourhoods being intimidated by those malcontents who make it their life's work to reinforce the aggressive stereotype of poverty. So Tallaght, to outsiders, was still perceived as the valley of the plague, a cast-out community of roughnecks and joy-riders, glue-sniffers and recidivist crooks.

'Much of the problem was that the new community coincided with the recession of the Seventies,' reflects Mary Sweeney of the Shanty Educational Project in Tallaght, 'and so there literally wasn't any money to provide services for the estates. But what we found was that more of the people coming in were young and energetic and keen to better themselves and they simply weren't going to tolerate having nothing. And the fact that we were far away from the centre of things meant we didn't slide into that lethargy of expecting handouts. We had to fight tooth and nail with the authorities for everything – schools, shops, a library, a community hall and now a third-level technical college and a proposed major hospital.' Suddenly the village of the plague was taking on a new meaning for the officials on the receiving end of any concentrated bout of Tallaght badgering. But anyone spending time in Tallaght today can be in no doubt that the people were right. However they wish to delude themselves, elected representatives, at either local or national level, exist to serve, not hinder or ignore, and it is to Tallaght's credit that it never ceases to remind the bureaucratic brotherhood of this first principle of public duty.

Not that things now happen easily, although with two junior Ministers (Mary Harney of the Progressive Democrats and Chris Flood of Fianna Fail) representing Tallaght in the Dail, the town's needs receive high-level attention. Even so, Mary Sweeney is probably right when she maintains that Tallaght citizens are too resourceful for their own good. 'I sometimes think that the authorities don't initiate anything here because they know they can leave it to us to get a task force moving.' Tom Hurley, unpaid voluntary public relations officer of the community council, agrees but with the qualification that Tallaght probably now wouldn't wish it any other way. It relishes the expertise it has developed in self-sufficiency and even thrives on a good fight with intransigent officials. As an indicator of a town pulling together it can list 147 voluntary groups; one of the two most distinguished Gaelic Athletic Association clubs in the country; a national reputation for marching bands; Tallaght Welfare Services, the community's leading voluntary social services agency which operates an extensive home-help system; two day-centres; a resources centre, and a Get Tallaght Working group. While Kiltalown House runs therapy courses and creativity programmes, the Shanty Education Project mainly promotes women's studies, and the Rock School provides training and facilities for youngsters wishing to test their potential as successors to Hot House Flowers and U2.

'There are about 5,500 unemployed here,' says Bob Byrne, 'and Tallaght will never be able to provide jobs for them, which gets us back to the need for better transport facilities. People must have ready access to the places where they can find work. Things have improved in the sense that we now have 18 routes in and out of the city centre, but the schedule is ridiculously planned. Nothing for ages and then a crop of them all together. We call them the banana buses because they come in bunches.'

With the commercial sophistication of The Square shopping mall now signifying Tallaght's coming of age, the community itself is more confident about voicing other worldly ambitions. Why should people have to go to Blessington for their wedding receptions? Why not build a smart hotel in Tallaght? Let's invite President Robinson to the Tallaght Personality of the Year dinner. And let's demand better landscaping and maintenance for Tallaght's parks. But also let's applaud the authorities when we can . . . to this end a letter was sent to Dublin County Council praising its recent refurbishment of the old village.

Rose O'Keeffe and Bridie Sweeney, both of Tallaght Welfare Society and former holders of the Personality of the Year award,

represent old Tallaght, their families having lived there for generations, passing on the social history, the ghost stories and that
vigorous Irish gossip at all manner of gatherings from funerals to
gab sessions around the fire. Both women brim with colourful
anecdotes and good nature, remembering the St Patrick's Days of
long ago when buses would bring the city folk out to the village of
Tallaght for their traditional picnics in the Dublin mountains.

'They would come in droves and as children we'd be so excited
watching them light their bonfires from the gorse,' says Bridie, 'and
some of them would be having such a good party they'd forget
about the time and catching the buses back, the last of which would
leave around ten p.m. And, mean little things that we were, we'd
jump out at them from behind the bushes and tell them that they'd
missed the bus. But they didn't mind because they were so happy.
They'd just set off and walk the miles to Dublin.'

Up the Old Bawn Road you can still gather blackberries from the
same brambles Rose and Bridie harvested as children. Mary
Sweeney, one of the first 'blow-ins' from Dublin 20 odd years ago,
says she never doubted Tallaght would be a marvellous place in
which to live after she caught sight of those blackberries – 'so big
and full of juice that they just fell off the branches. And wherever
you are in Tallaght you turn around and see a mountain.'

Today more than half Tallaght's residents own their own homes
and it shows not just in the number of privately built houses but
in the customer-choice front doors of local authority houses now
being purchased. But in the poorer neighbourhoods there is also
evidence of communal pride: a general trimness about the gardens
and people out shearing grass verges because the county council
cutters have failed to turn up.

This is still no trouble-free territory but unlike the housing
schemes of Glasgow's Easterhouse and Drumchapel, or Edinburgh's Pilton or London's Broadwater Farm (each one contami-
nated first by the town planners' sin of building a ghetto around
the socially deprived), West Tallaght's particular problems are not
indicated by vandalised phone booths or boarded-up windows or
Rottweilers being walked on the common greens. Even the graffiti
seems to have been applied with measured care. It comes in straight
lines, not hurled against the wall on violent impulse.

One asks if, like most other places, Tallaght has a drugs problem
and the universal answer is that hard drugs have not taken hold,

even if some of the youth have dabbled with hash. Bob Byrne recalls the day a drug-dealer rode into town. 'He was a very foolish feller obviously because he didn't understand what a tightly knit society we have here. Anyway, he came into town with a truck filled with coal and wood to make it look as if he were a merchant. He let it be known to some of the kids at the school that he'd be on the ground behind the health centre at seven that night.'

What he overlooked of course is that Tallaght is still a village. Word reached Bob Byrne at five p.m. and he went straight to the Guards, who picked the man up within ten minutes of seven o'clock. That story says something about Tallaght's own interpretation of Enterprise Culture, valiantly making inroads on outsiders' prejudices: turning round and seeing a mountain, but also finding the spunk to look beyond.

Tales of Old Tallaght 1: The Last Tram.

ON 1 AUGUST 1888, the first car of the new Dublin and Blessington Steam Tramway Co left Terenure at 8.45p.m. The first stop was at Templeogue and another stop at Tallaght. The actual stop was on Main Street. It continued, calling at Fox's Public House (now Jobstown House), then Embankment, Brittas, etc, finally reaching Blessington at 10.20a.m. Travelling from Terenure the fares were as follows: Templeogue Bridge: 6d first class, 5d third class. Tallaght: 11d and 9d, return 1/6d and 1/3d. These fares remained in operation up to about 1918, when Government control was enforced and fares were increased by 50 per cent and then 100 per cent.

A few years after the opening of the line, the Company was involved in litigation. A resident in the area sued the Company for damages, claiming that a spark from an engine had set his house on fire. The case was strongly contested, but the plaintiff won, and the Company paid up.

Within a year of the opening of the line, the first accident occurred at Templeogue, resulting in the death of a woman. There were many accidents and deaths in the following year. As these points were usually marked by a cross, the Dublin and Blessington Tramway was known locally as the longest graveyard in the world.

Wages: the drivers of the tram received 4/6d per day and firemen (or stokers as they were called) received 3/10d per day, for an 11-hour day.

The tram service was very popular at weekends and Bank holidays. This inspired a local poet to write a humorous poem about it, two lines of which ran as follows:

The battle of Ypres was only a sham
Compared to the rush for the Blessington Tram.

In 1913, efforts were made to induce the Great Southern Railways, and the Dublin United Tramways, to acquire the concern, but neither body appeared interested.

On Saturday, 31 December 1932, the last car to Tallaght left at 10.30p.m. Despite the night being wet, the tram carried a full complement of passengers. The run to Tallaght comprised one car, hauled by a locomotive, No 9. So, after 44 years of service, the Dublin to Blessington Tram was gone forever.

From The Dublin and Blessington Tramway *by H. Fayle and A. T. Newham.*

Tales from Old Tallaght 2: Wailing Walter

ONE OF THE VAST new housing areas of Greater Dublin is Kilnmanagh-Tallaght-Firhouse-Oldbawn. It is said that up to about 80 years ago the few hundred people who lived there were afraid to leave their homes after dark on certain nights – in case they met the ghost of a man who had cut his throat and died in a field between Tallaght and Oldbawn some years before. It was believed that bad luck would come to those who met the phantom.

The spectre was known locally as 'Wailing Walter' because it moaned loudly as it went on its nocturnal rambles. It was said to have been seen many times through the years near the field of death along the Tallaght-Oldbawn-Firhouse roads.

One man, however, was not unduly concerned. He was a local publican whose hobby was walking. One August evening he decided to visit a friend in Crumlin. It was quite dark when he headed for home. In the distance the bells of the Dominican Priory tolled midnight.

Suddenly he felt he was no longer alone – and then he saw walking beside him, step for step, a tall gaunt figure dressed in an overcoat that reached almost to his ankles. On his head he wore what looked like a deerstalker's cap.

He made no sound. There was no footfall and he did not reply when asked where he was headed. At a spot beyond the Greenhills Road, he turned up a lane, sobbing as he went. To his horror the publican saw that some drops of blood had fallen from the figure. He felt sick, panic overtook him. He half ran, half stumbled away from the spot.

Later he heard the story behind the ghost from a very old woman. Early in the 19th century, she said, a young gentleman, his wife and their 14-year-old daughter lived in a big house in the Tallaght district. The family butler and general man was Walter Watkins, who had worked for many years for the young man's father. He was devoted to the little girl but though an honest, hard-working chap, he had a liking for whiskey and would slip away to a tavern in Tallaght village.

On August Monday of 1806, the young people were invited to a party in Dublin. They gave strict instructions to the butler not to leave the house until they returned and to put their daughter to bed at seven o'clock. After he had tucked her up, he felt it would be safe to go to the village for an hour or so. He saddled a horse and went to meet his friends at the tavern, where he was soon making merry.

Time passed but, catching sight of the clock, he suddenly grew uneasy. He left immediately but when he returned he found his employer's daughter lying at the foot of the rambling staircase. An inquest revealed that she had apparently got out of bed to look for the butler, missed her footing on the stairs, and had fallen, breaking her neck.

The dreadful scene drove the butler insane. He ran screaming from the house and was found the next morning lying in a pool of blood in a field less than a quarter of a mile away. His throat had been cut and beside the body was a saddler's knife. Five days later a cowherd crossing the field saw a seated figure. He shouted a greeting – but the figure stood up and ran from the scene, wailing piteously. It was the ghost of Walter the Wailer!

Adapted from Ireland's Own.

20

VOICES
Jim Sheridan

MANGLED IN BODY and, to many ears, incomprehensible in speech, Christy Brown demanded the world's attention, then mocked it sometimes for the awkward admiring wonder it planted at his feet. When the demon was in him Brown could be as nippy as he was gifted and brave. But to those who loved him and to others who were more simply his friends the Dublin writer was not a cripple defying the muscles that betrayed his body because of cerebral palsy. For them he belonged to that school of cussed brilliance – a genius who knew his intellectual worth and who also knew how to charm and shatter simultaneously. One of 22 children (13 of whom survived) and raised in the working-class quarter of Kimmage on the outskirts of the capital, Brown was a man who, from the moment he propelled his wheelchair into company, could demolish any cant merchants present with an impish onslaught whether incoherent or not.

Several times during the Seventies, the last decade of his life, the film industry fiddled with the idea of turning his story into a movie. But Brown always scorned the crass notions that one or other of the box-office Richards (Burton or Harris) should play the leading role. What were the moguls looking for? Another Elephant Man or the Return of Quasimodo? Brown died in 1981 after choking on food. Some years earlier he had met and married the second most important woman in his life, Mary, a Kerry farmer's daughter working in London as a dental receptionist, and it was her handsome, calming presence which became crucial to his courage in ignoring handicap. She in fact continued the task of Brown's mother, a *mater dolorosa* who refused to consign her son to institutions, detecting in the grievous wreckage of the child a trapped intelligence and just a tremor of mobility. The single reliable limb in Christy Brown's body was his left foot, a limb through which – at his mother's boundless coaxing – he learned to paint and draw, to kick and manipulate a record player, and, on a typewriter, to converse or write the novels and poetry that sold throughout Europe, earning the kind of money no one – from his family to his publisher – could originally ever have imagined.

Christy Brown was right to resist the big film treatment. What took its place, *My Left Foot*, the movie of his first book, written in 1954, was very definitely the small treatment (made on a budget of just over three million dollars) but rendered heroic by a performance of unsqueamish honesty from Daniel Day Lewis which blazed with so much emotional force it took full possession of the audience. For those involved in the rights of the physically and mentally disabled this film's supportive value has been incalculable, but its dramatic worth also overtook the cinematic world and, indeed, completely 'winded' the hitherto unknown Irish team responsible for its direction and production. Ardent superlatives and international awards wreathed the film's showing from the start. By the time his Best Actor Oscar was announced in March 1990 Day Lewis, born in Ireland, had already picked up eight international awards for the role, including honours from the British Academy of Film and Television, the Montreal Film Festival and the New York Film Critics' Circle, which also voted *My Left Foot* best picture. In that year's Oscar categories the Dublin actress Brenda Fricker, who played Christy's mother, gained the Best Supporting Actress prize, and the movie was also nominated in many of the key sections (best picture, best director and best adapted screenplay). An exceptional achievement in any film buff's terms.

Cinematically *My Left Foot* may be faulty but for Jim Sheridan, the movie's director and co-scriptwriter with Shane Connaughton, its merit may well be unmatchable by the rest of his career. Already widely known in Dublin as a polemical theatre director Sheridan had never made a film before this one. Of the awards and nominations he simply exclaimed: 'Perhaps it's a bit much for a first film but all the same it's fantastic. What else can you say?' But Sheridan knew the glory was double-edged for it exerted additional pressures to create something extraordinary with *The Field*, his following film which, as it turned out, brought its leading player Richard Harris a Best Actor nomination in the 1991 Oscars' race. Sheridan had only met Christy Brown once or twice, but on each occasion he was impressed by the writer's massive energy. 'It was like watching a 747 prepare for lift-off,' he said. 'At once grounded and struggling for flight.'

The movie's producer, Noel Pearson, a fellow Dubliner and friend of Brown, had bought the film rights to the book and asked Sheridan to adapt it. 'I was immediately captured and, as I had been looking for a film, I asked Noel to let me direct it. Daniel seemed to me to be the obvious actor for the part and, just like the rest of us, as soon as he read the story he was hooked.' Day Lewis, emotionally and creatively drained at the tail-end of publicity tours for *The Unbearable Lightness of Being*, was just at the point of abandoning acting forever when the script arrived. It was, he says, the shove he had been waiting for, giving him back the desire to work, and in preparation he spent eight weeks at the Irish clinic where Brown had undergone therapy. 'For a couple of minutes on that first day,' he has said, 'I was overwhelmed by sadness. But then it just turned around when I realised that what I was feeling was the self-pity of an able-bodied person observing disability. When I actually looked at the kids there I saw extraordinary joy.'

Sheridan, always inspirational but taxing in the theatre, was no less demanding with *My Left Foot*, perhaps even more so as he was the novice on the film set. And enthused by the director's commitment to Brown's complicated character Day Lewis learned to paint with his foot and would spend up to ten hours a day in a wheelchair, his body twisted into Christy's contorted shape, his head lolling to one side and his speech no more than jumbled sounds. 'We were all greatly impressed,' recalls Sheridan wryly. 'Although a few of the crew felt it had gone beyond a joke when they had to feed him at mealtimes or haul him up three flights of ladders for some of the scenes.' For Sheridan, who is also artistic director of the Irish Arts Center in New York, much of the pleasure in working on the film came from the improbability of the subject. 'Because we were spared the hassle that comes with big financial backers we could just wrestle away with the complexities until we felt the movie was as right as possible.' But now, with two film commissions from Universal, he is considering the large, intricate theme of Irish emigration to America, one of his proposed stories concerning an Irishman who takes on the Mafia in the Thirties.

Both Sheridan and his brother Peter, also a theatre director, were born in Dublin and lived in Abercorn Road where Sean O'Casey also stayed. Their father began an amateur theatre group in 1969 to entertain old folk and it was this that encouraged his sons to look to drama for their careers. But neither has ever gone for the soft option by directing cosy, sentimental potboilers. At the Project Arts Centre in Dublin, where they worked from 1976 to 1980, Jim and Peter Sheridan were known as left-wing iconoclasts, exposing the raw nerves of politics or the sins respectable Dublin society preferred to leave muffled in the confessional – if indeed their admission ever got that far. Today Peter runs the City Centre, a spacious converted warehouse for community arts, situated on the other side of the Liffey, opposite the restored magnificence of James Gandon's Custom House, to many the most perfect example of 18th-century architecture in the city. The proximity of the two buildings is appropriate for the Sheridans epitomise a new, confident, original talent that while respecting the best from history is not daunted by past artistic glories.

Each of the brothers has worked in America over the years, finding its distance from home theatrically invigorating. 'I initially went to the States because I thought it would be a big trap for an Irish person to go to England,' says Jim. The English, he reflects, insist that Dubliners speak the best English in the world. 'They don't but they may speak the most entertaining English. They speak with hyperbole and circumlocution while the English speak directly.' And if powerful money is now buttressing a revived film industry in Ireland Jim Sheridan is not automatically worrying that creative freedoms will be weakened. 'People say that this can be corrupting, but the point is to use success to strengthen your own terms.' Anchored in his wheelchair, Christy Brown repeatedly upheld that kind of sentiment. He called it a better-than-death-wish.

21

SCENES
The DART

ON THAT DAY, some time ago, when the sea froze at Salthill and the wind whipped snow into steep bobsleigh walls at Killiney, the DART disappeared from the tracks at Dalkey, leaving many of County Dublin's thrusting achievers jabbering on the platform from under their tweeds and waxed jackets about the incompetence of public transport.

'One blizzard and they're banjaxed,' ranted a Barboured careerist. 'They retreat indoors without even having the decency to inform us that the entire service is cancelled.' As he continued to vent his bad humour others around him set forth to yomp to work through drifts and abandoned cars, turning their backs on the DART, an acronym for Dublin Area Rapid Transport, and a name which has led many a wag to proclaim that: 'Isn't it a good thing now that Dublin wasn't called Florence?'

It was round about Dun Laoghaire, on that deep-freeze day, that a female executive, adventurously attired in a ski suit of geranium pink, suddenly heard the smooth hum of the DART's overhead electric cables and in no time she saw one train slowly glide along, the passengers comfortably ensconced with their morning newspapers and Nanook-of-the-North ensembles. Some minutes later as she slithered on all fours towards the city, there it was again, the gentle rumour of a DART catching her right ear-muff. And sure enough, a train skimmed past with all the optimism of a chartered picnic outing. The driver even had the cheek to wave. In response, the ski-suited female executive jumped up and down, shook one fist, then two, whereupon the driver stopped the DART, opened his cab window and called up the embankment: 'In heaven's name what ails you, woman?'

'You ail me,' came the reply. 'Haven't I just wasted one hour and a half of my life standing at Dalkey station for a DART, and no sooner do I move off to crawl my way to work than two trains overtake me in slow succession.'

'Arragh, even if ye'd still been standing there, we wouldn't have picked you up,' the driver soothed. 'There are no trains at all pulling into Dalkey today. It's limited stops only in order to keep some semblance of order on the line.'

At this point the female executive chanced her luck. 'Listen, would you ever let me hitch a lift as far as the city?'

'Well,' considered the driver gravely, 'given the vicious nature of the day that's in it, and the possibility of you're being able to throw the two legs over the railings, then, begod, I'll chance it.'

So the female executive threw the legs over the iron fence, followed by the rest of her, then slid down the embankment to arrive at the driver's cab door on her bottom. Unceremoniously he hauled her in, cajoling her never to give out about the indifference of public transport officials again, and then he opened the second door into the carriages, allowing the stowaway to join the bona fide travellers.

That morning, by the time the female executive reached her premises, Mr Tom, the commissionaire, was already up to his elbows in a new role. On Monday, he had suggested whimsically that in view of the snow storms the staff might like to lunch inside the office. If so, he would be very happy to pop around the corner and bring in a chicken. Everyone had agreed that this was a very sensible arrangement and so Mr Tom had returned with a suitable bird, plus stuffing accompaniments and a few pounds of best potatoes.

The miracle was that while he never appeared to be missing from the office lobby, neither did he seem to skimp his time in the tiny upstairs kitchen next to the management suite, and the chicken had been so successful that by next day a lunch kitty had been organised. On Tuesday Mr Tom had entertained the staff to a slowly simmered stew. On Wednesday he had borrowed a cookery book and was studying the best joints of beef. As far as anyone could tell, this was the first week in his life that Mr Tom had turned his hand to cooking. In pursuit of the art and on detecting the closing moments of a discussion with a client he would now approach the female executive with his courteous, velvet tread, and whisper: 'I wonder if I might interrupt for just one second. Will there be the usual nine for luncheon today?'

This diversion from commercial matters, far from irritating the departing client, seemed to instil a gentle pleasure, even the feeling that despite new-fangled technology, here was proof that his business remained in trusty, old-fangled hands. Towards the end of the week the DART had returned to normal, journeying back and forth between Bray and Howth in that great salty coastal arc which must be one of the most enchanting and therapeutic commuter runs in Europe. And, this being Dublin, even the posters above the seats respect the written word: home-bound workers glance up at Gerard Manley Hopkins's *Moonrise* in the DART's Poetry in Motion series, and everyone observes the directive, forbidding 'feet on the seat'.

By Thursday, though, the cordon bleu office was well on the way to becoming a habit. The female executive was now being asked to oversee the gravy, and by Friday the culinary commissionaire was preparing roast pork with apple sauce, followed by plum tart and custard. But then this sort of thing probably happens all the time in Dublin, for Ireland remains the kind of small, intimate country where initiative is still comradely and informal, emerging at a relaxed pace rather than with any angry stamping of the foot. The thaw might have begun, yet what of it? Momentarily away from the solemn front door of the premises, Mr Tom was upstairs with his apron on, contemplating duck à l'orange.

22

VOICES
Beckett

FOR MORE THAN half his lifetime Samuel Beckett lay in wait to catch death on the threshold, and death played hard to get. But when it arrived at a festive weekend, the old immobilist, conscious or not, would have been ready, chuckling even that an agnostic, born on a Good Friday the 13th, should have panted on until Christmas 1989, some 83 years later, turning the liturgical calendar on its head. Samuel Beckett was not a pessimist but he was the black hole inside every person's psyche; that dark, tormented corner where we lose ourselves in fear of loneliness and decrepitude, in not just a dread of dying but the terror of being forgotten. His work, from *Molloy* and *Malone Dies* onwards, seems often no more than a bleak, amputated whisper, but the impact can be horrifying in its brave depiction of man's fall from grace and the savage grasp of absurdity.

'Let me say before I go any further that I forgive nobody . . . I wish them all an atrocious life and then the fires and ice of hell . . .' There is something ferociously Irish in the curse Beckett allows Malone, yet to what nationality does his literature belong? Born in the Foxrock neighbourhood of Dublin to middle-class Protestant parents, he escaped the Ascendancy tag and its self-improving temperance by moving to Paris in the Thirties, after working as a lecturer at Trinity College. On the Left Bank Beckett became both an acolyte and friend of James Joyce and a crucial figure in the radical and frequently impecunious bohemia of the day.

189

Anthony Burgess describes him as 'a French writer' – one who, according to Sartre, 'has written the most distinguished French prose of the century'. Beckett's English scholars, of course, would claim him as their prize and indeed more books about him have been written in English than about any other contemporary dramatist in history. But the writer Edna O'Brien detects the 'fibulations' of Ireland in him. 'Whether he writes in English or French his voice is indisputably Irish and his mental landscape recalls those bare, exigent and endless acres of limestone that are to be found in the Burren in County Clare.'

Like Joyce, though, Beckett kicked free of his native land's throttling conformity by becoming a self-imposed exile, never returning to Dublin again after 1968. 'A vicious crowd,' he called the Irish. Nevertheless, as the erudite Eoin O'Brien observed in his exquisitely illustrated book, *The Beckett Country*, Foxrock Village, Dublin and its mountains and sea coast, and the fine family home, Cooldrinagh, at the junction of Kerrymount Avenue and Brighton Road, never entirely disappeared from Beckett's mindscape. Instead their presence lapped against his early prose work and the later writing, too. Moran's house in *Molloy*, notes Dr O'Brien, is based on Cooldrinagh, 'where the scene is idyllic but threatened'.

> *None but tranquil sounds, the clicking of the mallet and ball, a rake on pebbles, a distant lawn-mower, the bell of my beloved church. And birds of course, blackbird and thrush, their song sadly dying, vanquished by the heat, and leaving dawn's high bows for the bushes' gloom. Contentedly I inhaled the scent of my lemon-verbena. In such surroundings slipped away my last moments of peace and happiness.*

In *How It Is* Beckett also cherishes a spring recollection of Leopardstown Racecourse which was a few minutes' walk from Foxrock railway station:

> *we are if I may believe the colours that deck the emerald grass if I may believe them we are old dream of flowers and seasons we are in April or May and certain accessories if I may believe them white rails a grandstand colour of old rose we are on a racecourse in April or May*

Yet despite Beckett's exasperation with his countrymen, his disownment of what Edna O'Brien calls 'the unctious gombeen, crubeen twilightis mistakenly thought to be Celtic', he knew his work was never better served than when it was streaming out of the mouths of two of them: the actors Jack MacGowran (with whom Beckett worked most closely on the role of Lucky in *Waiting for Godot*) and Patrick Magee for whom he wrote *Krapp's Last Tape*.

Just as he shunned explanations of his work, so he disliked those performers who tried to interpret it, but for many the low but panic-stricken rhythms of the speeches have often presented problems. MacGowran observed: 'Every time I've seen *Godot*, Lucky's great speech (perhaps what goes through everybody's mind at the verge of death) has been a jumble and you couldn't make anything out of it because it was delivered so quickly. But this needn't be the case. When Beckett was trying to explain the rhythm to me he recorded Lucky's speech on a tape recorder and I listened to that many, many times. It's really one long sentence that ends with the conclusion that man wastes and pines, wastes and pines.'

In appearance Beckett looked like a figure carved from the old stones of his literary terrain. Tall and beaky, he was thin like a shard of slate, and his pale blue eyes were lodged beneath a formidable cliff of bone. This physical austerity intimidated many but it also served him well when in 1937 he was stabbed close to the heart by a passing pimp on the Avenue d'Orleans in Paris, and later when he was in the French Resistance and miraculously escaped the Gestapo. The famed reclusive nature also had its lighter side. Beckett was always courteous and an attentive listener to those meeting him for the first time, his stern face losing its eager gaze whenever he permitted it to smile. Peggy Guggenheim, patron and predator of the Paris existentialist movement, claimed a torrid liaison with the playwright. They had met as James Joyce's Christmas guests at Fouquet's in 1937. And Peggy found herself fascinated by 'the young, lean man with huge, blue-green eyes that stared straight ahead with pinpoint precision'. He walked her to her borrowed apartment on the rue de Lille. She asked him indoors. And Beckett in return sheepishly asked her to lie down beside him on the sofa. 'We soon found ourselves in bed where we remained until the next evening,' she recounted noisily to her circle. 'We might be there still but I had to go and dine with Arp [*the sculptor*] who unfortunately had no telephone.' When Beckett finally left after having dashed out to buy champagne which the two polished off between the sheets he simply offered the inscrutable comment: 'Thank you, it was nice while it lasted.'

Up to his death, however, Beckett always defied the academic industry that has foisted itself on to his work. He remained an enigma, confounding analysis, calling his writing 'a stain upon the silence' and describing his 80-odd years as 'dull and without interest – the professors know more about it than I do'. Above all, though, he is the Nobel laureate whose effect on world literature is assured by his sense of dislodgement and the babble of words which have given spare but superbly cadenced expression to desolation and monotony: 'The sun shone, having no alternative on nothing new.' That line at the start of *Murphy* conveys much of life's absurdity but a belief that it is harsh and often without purpose. Beckett's characters talk to obliterate the snarling sadness of wrecked hope, wrecked words: 'Ever tried. Ever failed. No matter. Try again. Fail again. Fail better . . .' Beckett dies, and Malone, Murphy, Godot and the rest of them haunt us forever.

23

ENVOI
Dun Laoghaire

IN THE LATE 1850s, long before travel dwindled into tourism, a gentleman staying overnight in a hotel on Dublin's Westland Row would request a call at six in the morning so as to prepare himself, in leisurely fashion, for his voyage by rail and sea to Britain. On awaking his bath would be drawn and as a gentle breakfast was being served he might read his newspapers and maybe light up a cigar. Then he would summon the concierge to have his bags carried over to the station, and, within 15 minutes, the gentleman would be out on the East Pier at Kingstown, stepping, without care or fluster, directly from the train on to the boat. A porter, his subtle palm decently tipped, would have brought the luggage to the cabin, and in under three hours the voyager would be disembarking at Holyhead to begin his round of equally well-planned appointments.

Such is the sly nature of progress that the Sealink ferry service now plying between the British mainland and Dun Laoghaire (the old Gaelic name having been re-instated in 1922) takes longer than the slender paddle steamer of our good gentleman's day. Not only that, the railway line which deposited him so tidily at the gangway no longer runs right to the wharf, so passengers arriving by train must stumble along, ambushed every few yards by their own luggage, until they reach the boarding gates. Most travellers, of course, will have come by car which explains why, in the myopic eyes of contemporary traffic planners, pedestrians count for nothing. And yet if there is an Irish paradise for walkers this is

193

it, this stretch of Dublin Bay where neighbouring Monkstown, Blackrock, Sandycove and Dalkey all seem to converge in a permanent promenade around Dun Laoghaire's splendid harbour. They are not the only ones to take the air. Along the shoreline towards Sandycove cormorants have taken up squatters' rights on the rocks and are hanging out their black umbrella wings to dry. A primeval heron stands on the water, his beak at the ready like a rifle. By evening a family of playful seals may have commandeered the outer rocks but just now oyster catchers, red shanks and ringed plover are scampering amid the pebbles and the kelp, inebriated with chatter.

In the early afternoon on Sunday the walking pace of the East Pier of Dun Laoghaire is almost competitive. There are small groups of intense Chekhovian strollers but on the whole the wind has little patience with amblers, pushing them down into the collars of their coats to take shelter in the lee of the lighthouse which, every 30 seconds, flings its brilliant wand out across the sea. In clear visibility you can see that beam of warning and welcome from a distance of 25 miles, and nearly opposite the beacon, on the extreme promontory of Howth Head, there is the Baily Lighthouse, then away out, the Kish lightship guarding the vicinity in which the mailboat *Leinster* sank after being torpedoed by a German submarine on 10 October 1918. The death toll was appalling: 501 people perished but 256 were saved by British destroyers and returned to Dun Laoghaire. And as in most ports when tragedy strikes, nearly everyone had a connection with those directly wounded by that night. Seaside towns, as much as they are rooted in old fashioned pleasures, are tagged with reminders of mortality: lifebuoys hung like wreaths on the walls; Swimming Prohibited notices, and on the East Pier, a monument to Captain Boyd and the crew of the *Ajax* who were drowned while attempting to save the lives of some ship-wrecked mariners in the great gale of February 1861. Thirty-four years later a violent storm ripped Christmas Eve asunder, killing Dun Laoghaire's lifeboat men during their fruitless attempt to retreive sailors from a sinking Norwegian barque. On Marine Parade a simple obelisk commemorates their bravery.

But all this makes Dun Laoghaire sound too melancholy. Back on the East Pier the genteel gaiety of the place is signalled by a graceful anemometer which has recorded wind speed and direction since the 1850s. Dun Laoghaire dates from the reign of Laoghaire, the high king of Ireland at the time that St Patrick began his missionary labours among the people in 432. Designating the land between De Vesci Gardens and the harbour as his fort, the king became the first in a legendary line of nobles to be converted by Patrick. Even so he didn't go reverently to meet his Maker. Laoghaire squeezed the very last breath from his body to direct his warriors to bury him eternally facing his lifelong foes, the Leinstermen.

In the 18th century the town was scarcely more than a fishing village and it was Dalkey's Coliemore Harbour, a few minutes along the coast to the South, which cornered the trade from fat mercantile vessels whose tradition of tying up there dated, in fact, from the 1300s. But Dun Laoghaire's outlook was majestically altered when the British Exchequer delved into its colonial purse to provide close on £1 million for the building of two massive pincer-shaped piers in 1817. What emerged from the design of the great Scots engineer John Rennie still stands unparalleled in naval architecture and is, quite simply, one of the most handsome stone harbours in the whole of Europe. Essentially built to accommodate the Empire's warships and also speed the mail facilities of the package boats travelling between Ireland and England, each curving limb of the construction is composed of beautifully cut granite blocks, hewn from the Dalkey quarries. By 1834 the first railway line in Ireland was terminating at Dun Laoghaire's door, bringing not only seafarers but the new merchants and the old merchants from Dublin, keen to take the waters and, eventually, settle their families in the custom-built villas of De Vesci Terrace, Sydenham Terrace and Clarinda Park. Today the town's ornamental scrolling and ironwork and those improbable stucco lions lazing about on domestic rooftops are among the legacies of that exuberance and here, too, the Irish delight in colourful façades spills over on to the villas which nestle intimately into one another rather than stand loftily apart. Right along the bay whole houses are wonderfully bathed in washes of coral, ochre, salmon pinks, a buttery cream, flint grey and chalky blue.

In a disarmingly unofficial sort of way Peter Pearson, the Dun Laoghaire painter, has become its urgent janitor of artefacts, an inspired caretaker of the town. By campaigning whenever and wherever he can Pearson husbands both history and masonry against the brutish foolery of planners, and he is right to be jumping up and down on others' toes. Following on from the discarded in-fill project for the West Pier one more proposal has arisen which would develop the town as a ferry port and turn a substantial chunk of the harbour into the rich man's marina playground. Pearson is no whingeing purist seeking the élitism of changing nothing so that only vehement environmentalists have a say, but he does question the communal benefit of turning much of this wild and lovely arm of the harbour into a yacht club for the privileged; a common amenity suddenly ruled by bull-necked watchmen at steel gates, and those highly strung committees that harangue the members' dining room with arcane regulations on dress. Pearson has a story about this. Some years ago he was taken to lunch at one of Dun Laoghaire's four existing yacht clubs and he turned up in the sweater and jeans of the working artist. There were frowns at the door and much strained clearing of throats before he was asked discreetly if perhaps he wouldn't mind changing into something a touch more formal. Not wishing to embarrass his lunch guest he dashed home, home being not far along the road, and climbed into the best he could find: a tailcoat, picked up at a thrift shop, which he then stylishly accessorised with a crash helmet and bow tie. Suppressing their confusion the honorifics let him in, and, just to prove he, too, was a gentleman, Pearson placed his helmet underneath the table.

Ten years ago Peter Pearson wrote a book on Dun Laoghaire in which he lovingly detailed its ornamental character and distinction, its Gothic spires, Victorian bay window terraces, its evocations of Venetian palaces and its occasional air of neo-classical importance. The book, named after the town, is to be reprinted but since he wrote it there has been talk of redeveloping the Pavilion corner, and his heart sinks for the proposal offers a multi-sports complex of hangar dimensions softened only slightly by some stone embellishment. The original turn-of-the-century building possessed a soaring sense of festivity but all that stands there now is the concrete heap of a condemned cinema. What is needed, Pearson believes, is a replacement which doesn't ape the past or root up all the grand old trees or, indeed, dwarf the superb Italianate town hall opposite. Instead he advocates a building sensitively designed in the modern idiom yet still capturing the first construction's joyful grace. Let it include a theatre, a cinema and a roof garden restaurant for all the people, for it is a curious thing that Dun Laoghaire today owns none of these enticements. There is Teddy's famous ice cream shop on the front, one or two fast-food cafés in the town's dismal shopping centre and a posh eaterie in the stately shell of the old station. But no tea shop and no coffee house.

Are Dun Laoghaire's inhabitants too sniffy for such delights? Pearson doesn't think so. The station building, he feels sure, could be turned into the most enjoyable kind of brasserie, a meeting point through the day and night for people already entranced by harbour lights and the bustle on the pier. After all, the French regard the brasserie as one of the natural components of civilised living. Yet more proposed outcrops of concrete acne will no doubt be strenuously opposed by the public, but Pearson feels the townsfolk also need to be energised into thinking imaginatively about Dun Laoghaire's future. Otherwise the entire place, with a population of 60,000, will end up either as a museum or an under-funded Celtic Puerto Banus.

As we walk along Marine Parade Pearson points out two monuments which came in for blasts of extreme political vandalism. The first is the Victoria fountain, 'a defenceless relic of the past' which was made in a foundry in Glasgow and lost its elaborate canopy and sovereign's head in 1981 when its was detonated by the IRA. Further along, the tapering granite pillar called the George 1V Testimonial still stands like a colonial imperative. Fifteen years or so ago a bunch of militants, trying to destroy it, only managed to rob it of one of its spheres, but in this instance they might have had an unlikely ally in William Thackeray who, during a visit to Dun Laoghaire in 1874, described the monument as 'a hideous obelisk stuck on four fat balls'. Near the oldest boat slip in the harbour we reach one of Pearson's favourite buildings, the lifeboathouse which was constructed in 1862 as a memorial to the crew which had drowned the year before. Newly and painstakingly restored, it resembles a little Greek temple in Pearson's view with its quartz keystone picked out in finely chiselled lines.

There is a man in Dalkey called Frank Burke who, some time ago, wrote a letter to the *Irish Times* on the emotive topic of dog droppings. The amount of such waste on the paths of beautiful Dalkey village, he said, never failed to amaze and annoy him. In fact Mr Burke reflected that he could not walk ten paces without meeting a dog dropping. 'It's bad enough going down to the pub at night – I can zig and zag around them then. But coming back at closing time is a different matter.' What could be done? After much consideration Mr Burke hit on an enterprising answer: 'Dog nappies. That's it. Disposable, of course. Specially designed, with an aperture for the tail, and made in three sizes – large, medium and small. There would have to be right-legged and left-legged ones, depending on which rear limb your dog lifts when passing the lamp posts and my car tyres. More freedom on the lifting side . . .' Being a realist Mr Burke felt himself too old to market his invention but he was floating it so that some young entrepreneur could seize the challenge and turn himself into a millionaire. 'If he does, all I ask is that he gives me a present of a fully grown elephant, which I would probably lead around Dalkey. Without a nappy, of course, and that would teach the lot of yeh . . .'

At the time of my last visit to Dalkey there was not a single dog dropping underfoot. Either the canine owners had been shamed into better behaviour by the Burke initiative or else it was because this was Good Friday when dogs in Christian Dalkey probably do their business elsewhere as a final act of Lenten penance. Anyway, it was the best of times to see this engaging tangle of sloping streets with little prettified cottages and imposing villas rising steeply towards wooded hills. In this first sustained shaft of sunshine lawns, studded with palm trees and blossoming bushes, were polished to a juicy green, and at Coliemore Harbour the doors of the small blue fishermen's huts were thrown back to admit the fine weather, revealing the age-old indispensable tackle of those who brave a living from the sea. As my friend and I walked back to Sandycove briny stoics were plunging into the Forty Foot, that foaming well of water cragged with rocks where, by tradition, gentlemen once defied Ireland's reputation for prudery by swimming naked in all seasons. What passes for equal opportunity seems to have put paid to that, for, since the time women bathers were grudgingly given the right to dive in, too, a prissy notice has appeared declaring: TOGS MUST BE WORN WHEN SWIMMING. The Forty Foot derives its name from the 40th Regiment of Foot which was stationed in a battery above it, and to the left that day the first of the season's French tourists were photographing James Joyce's museum, the squat Martello fortress occupied in *Ulysses* by 'stately, plump Buck Mulligan' and friends. Next door the white nautical shape of a house designed by the distinguished Dublin architect Michael Scott picks up the tower's abundant curve, and looks out to sea, like a moored Corbusier liner.

DUN LAOGHAIRE

In the evening the promenaders were still on the East Pier, up and down, up and down with tremendous mileage to their credit. Even so they are not rovers in the way that the crowd on the West Pier are, gallivanting along its grassy reaches to take their minds off the ice in the wind. The East Pier carries thousands of walkers each year, although many of them must be the same fellow retracing his steps. Yet there is a rhythmical and pleasing solidarity about this traipsing, and it brings with it fascinating breeze-borne snips of conversation: 'Howya, Michael . . . tell me is your sister still in the cats and dogs home?' Men with binoculars gaze endlessly, gull-watching or ship-spotting, and earnest fishermen try their luck next to angling urchins. Soon the mailboat will be underway, its blazing lights and farewell hoots of the siren adding glamour to all this tidal restlessless. In the morning foghorns from the mist may guide its return. And so it has been for generations . . . a boat with no mail now, only cars and people being carried emotionally away from Dublin, and back again, on the glitter of the sea.

APPENDIX

A

The League of Small Nations

THE LEAGUE OF SMALL NATIONS

	Austria	Denmark	Finland	Ireland	NZ	Norway	Switz	UK
Population *(millions)*...	7.6	5.1	4.9	3.5	3.3	4.2	6.7	57.0
GDP per head *($US)*...	12.5	13.7	13.8	8.1	11.0	15.9	16.6	13.4
EMPLOYMENT *(% of labour force)*								
Agriculture...............	8.1	5.8	9.8	15.4	10.4	6.4	5.7	2.3
Industry	37.4	27.2	30.6	27.8	26.4	26.4	35.1	29.3
Services	54.5	67.1	59.6	56.8	63.6	67.1	59.2	68.0
LIVING STANDARDS *(per 1000 inhabitants)*								
Cars	370	321	344	201	490	388	419	318
Phones.....................	460	783	615	235	646	622	1334	521
TV sets......................	300	392	370	181	291	346	337	336
PROJECTIONS—Growth in GNP/GDP *(% change on previous year)*								
1988	3.9	−0.2	5.4	1.4	1.7	1.2	3.0	4.6
1989	4.0	1.4	5.2	5.0	0.8	5.0	3.1	2.2
1990	4.5	1.0	1.7	4.4	0.7	3.0	2.5	1.6
1991	2.9	0.8	0.0	3.2	1.5	3.2	2.0	0.7
1992	2.9	2.1	1.2	3.1	2.3	2.7	1.8	1.9
UNEMPLOYMENT *(% of labour force)*								
1988	3.6	8.6	4.6	16.7	5.6	3.2	0.7	7.8
1989	3.2	9.3	3.5	15.6	6.8	5.1	0.6	7.5
1990	3.3	9.6	8.3	14.0	7.6	5.3	0.6	8.1
1991	3.3	10.2	8.9	13.9	7.6	5.1	0.7	9.4
1992	3.3	9.9	9.4	13.7	7.4	4.9	0.7	9.4
INFLATION *(GDP deflator, % change on previous period)*								
1988	2.2	4.2	7.0	3.3	8.6	3.7	2.5	6.7
1989	2.9	4.4	6.7	4.9	5.9	4.9	3.3	6.9
1990	3.5	3.3	6.5	3.6	4.4	3.6	4.5	5.8
1991	4.0	3.7	5.7	3.2	3.3	3.2	4.9	6.7
1992	3.4	3.2	4.7	3.3	3.0	3.3	3.9	5.6

Source: OECD Economic base figures are for 1988, though some figures for living standards are for earlier years.

APPENDIX

B

Note on Sources

PRINCIPAL SOURCES

INTERVIEWS

Ballagh, Robert
Bolger, Dermot
Byrne, Gay
Durcan, Paul
FitzGerald, Garret
Harney, Mary
Lenihan, Brian
Linehan, Rosaleen
McCarthy, Muriel

Mortell, Michael
Pearson, Peter
Robinson, President Mary
Rocha, John and Odette
Sheridan, Jim
Sheridan, Peter
Treacy, Father Bernard
Whisker, Charlie and Mariad

BOOKS

Banned in Ireland: Censorship and the Irish Writer. Edited by Julia
   Carlson. (Routledge, 1990)
Brendan Behan's Ireland. By Brendan Behan. (Hutchinson, 1962)
Church and State in Modern Ireland 1923-1979. By J.H. Whyte. (Gill &
   Macmillan)
Culture & Anarchy in Ireland 1890-1939. By F.S.L. Lyons. (Oxford, 1979)
Daughters of Erin. By Elizabeth Coxhead. (Secker & Warburg, 1965)
Dublin, a Capital City. (Lloyd's of London Press, 1988)
Dublin. By V.S. Pritchett. (The Bodley Head, 1967; the Hogarth Press,
   1991)

Dublin Quartet: Plays by Dermot Bolger. (Penguin, 1991)

Dun Laoghaire: Kingstown. By Peter Pearson. (The O'Brien Press, 1981)

Economic Outlook. OECD. (Paris, 1991)

Ireland, a Social and Cultural History. By Terence Browne. (Fontana, 1981)

Joyce: The Man, the Work, the Reputation. By Marvin Magalaner and Richard M. Kain. (Plantin, 1956)

No Laughing Matter: The Life and Times of Flann O'Brien. By Anthony Cronin. (Grafton Books, 1989)

Patrick Kavanagh: The Complete Poems. (The Goldsmith Press, 1984)

Religious Practice and Attitudes in Ireland 1988-89. By Micheal Mac-Greil. (St Patrick's College, Maynooth, 1991)

Terrible Beauty. A Life of Constance Markievicz. By Diana Norman. (Hodder & Stoughton, 1987)

The Beckett Country. By Eoin O'Brien. (Faber, 1986)

The Crozier & the Dail: Church & State 1922-1988. By John Cooney. (The Mercier Press, 1986)

The Dynamics of Irish Politics. By Paul Bew, Ellen Hazelkorn, and Henry Patterson. (Lawrence & Wishart, 1989)

The Selected Paul Durcan. Edited by Edna Langley. (The Blackstaff Press, 1982)

The Spirit of the Nation: The Speeches of Charles M. Haughey. Edited by Martin Mansergh. (The Mercier Press, 1986)

The Ulysses Guide: Tours through Joyce's Dublin. By Robert Nicholson. (Methuen, 1988)

Ultimate Dublin Guide. By Brian Lalor. (The O'Brien Press, 1991)

Understanding Contemporary Ireland: State, Class and Development in the Republic of Ireland. By Richard Breen, Damian F. Hannan, David B. Rottman and Christopher T. Whelan. (Gill and Macmillan, 1990)

Women in Ireland. By Jenny Beale. (Macmillan, 1986)

NEWSPAPERS

Irish Times

Irish Independent

Irish Press

Glasgow Herald

Sunday Independent

Sunday Tribune

The Observer

INDEX

INDEX